She Had Told Him All About Herself,

but what did she re...

"You're a bi... You leave here at ... ...lace I can't picture ... do . . . *whatev...* ...n. When Monday comes I don't d... ...ask for fear you'll get angry. I know you were married, but I don't dare ask about your wife or where you lived or where you learned to design the way you do." She looked at him gently, beseechingly. *"Can* I ask you those things? Would you answer me?"

He looked at her and realized all that he wanted to tell her. Yet there was still one part of him that held back, one part that feared he would be lost. If he confided in her he would be totally vulnerable.

BILLIE DOUGLASS

enjoys writing romances and confesses that her "family, friends, and imagination" influence what ultimately comes from her typewriter. She spends hours at the library researching (backseat traveling) new and interesting locations. Ms. Douglass lives with her husband and three sons in Massachusetts.

Dear Reader,

Silhouette Special Editions are an exciting new line of contemporary romances from Silhouette Books. Special Editions are written specifically for our readers who want a story with heightened romantic tension.

Special Editions have all the elements you've enjoyed in Silhouette Romances and *more*. These stories concentrate on romance in a longer, more realistic and sophisticated way, and they feature greater sensual detail.

I hope you enjoy this book and all the wonderful romances from Silhouette.

Karen Solem
Editor-in-Chief
Silhouette Books

BILLIE DOUGLASS
The Carpenter's Lady

Silhouette Special Edition
Published by Silhouette Books New York
America's Publisher of Contemporary Romance

SILHOUETTE BOOKS, a Division of Simon & Schuster, Inc.
1230 Avenue of the Americas, New York, N.Y. 10020

Distributed by Pocket Books

ISBN: 0-671-53633-8

First Silhouette Books printing December, 1983

10 9 8 7 6 5 4 3 2 1

Map by Ray Lundgren

SILHOUETTE, SILHOUETTE SPECIAL EDITION and
colophon are registered trademarks of Simon & Schuster, Inc.

America's Publisher of Contemporary Romance

Printed in the U.S.A.

Other Silhouette Books by Billie Douglass

Search for a New Dawn
A Time to Love
Knightly Love
Sweet Serenity
Fast Courting
Flip Side of Yesterday
Beyond Fantasy
An Irresistible Impulse

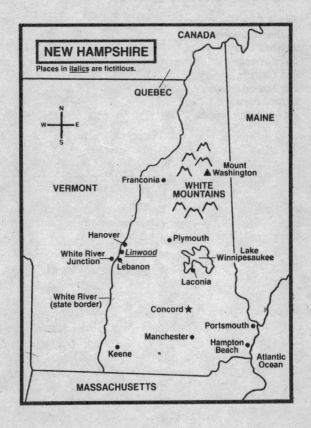

NEW HAMPSHIRE

Places in <u>italics</u> are fictitious.

CANADA

QUEBEC

MAINE

N
W — E
S

Mount
▲ Washington

Franconia ●

WHITE
MOUNTAINS

VERMONT

Hanover
White River
Junction

Linwood

Lebanon

● Plymouth

Lake
Winnipesaukee

White River
(state border)

Laconia

Concord ★

Portsmouth ●

Manchester ●

Hampton
Beach

Keene ●

Atlantic
Ocean

MASSACHUSETTS

Chapter One

*F*rom the waist down, he was promising. His jeans fit him like the hide of a lion, gliding over hard muscle as he twisted on the dolly beneath the truck in search of an elusive valve. Weathered from wear, the denim traversed a rangy path from the worn leather of his belt to that of his work boots. When he bent one knee up in an attempt to lever himself properly, the muscle of his other thigh tensed, drawing the faded material taut.

Feeling like the voyeur she'd never been, Debra Barry cleared her throat. "Excuse me? Graham Reid?" When the topless body made no move to respond, she stepped closer and bent from the waist to assure herself that there was indeed a man above the lean hips beneath the truck in the service-station bay. "Hello?"

His wrench hit the cement with a soft clang as he muttered an oath. Straightening his torso, he used his flexed leg to guide the dolly forward. With the emerging of a chest, shoulders and head, Debra found herself face to face with the man she'd been sent to see. He was dirty, with streaks of grime on his face and hands and on his forearms where the sleeves of his heavy wool shirt had been rolled back. That, too, had seen cleaner days, as had his hair, a shaggy thatch that cleared his forehead only by virtue of his still-prone position. But his eyes were clear, clear and amber, staring at her as though she'd personally sabotaged his truck.

"Yes?" came his voice, deep and remarkably impassive.

"I'm looking for Graham Reid," she returned in relief. At least he hadn't lashed out at her as those eyes had hinted he might have done. But then, this was New Hampshire, not New York. This was a rural man, not a city man. His temperament would be that much more even. She'd have to remember that.

"Yes."

She raised a brow in anticipation. "You're Graham Reid?"

"Yes." This time his voice was firmer and bore a note of impatience. With his hands grasping the footboard of the truck above his head, he continued to stare at her.

Debra took a deep breath. "I need a carpenter. You've been recommended. I wonder if we might talk."

When the man simply continued to stare, she wondered if she'd somehow offended him. Had it not been for his eyes, she might have suspected that he hadn't understood her request. But those eyes were sharp, looking at nothing but her face, yet seeming to see everything at once. Suddenly, she grew self-conscious.

"You *are* a carpenter, aren't you?" she queried in frustration. "Or is it your father . . . or some other Graham Reid whose work I've seen?"

The man on the ground blinked as though brought back from a daydream, then gave a shove with his hands, rolled free of the truck and stood in one fluid move. Debra half-wished he'd remained on the ground. If she'd thought that his eyes were intimidating, she hadn't counted on his superior height or the commanding breadth of his chest and shoulders.

"You've seen my work?" he demanded in that same level voice.

"Yes. I made stops at both the Hardys' and the Lavelles' before I came looking for you. There seemed little point in taking your time or mine to talk," she reasoned, "if I didn't like your work to begin with." A flash of something akin to respect passed through his gaze, though it was gone so quickly she half-suspected she'd imagined it.

Graham Reid rubbed his hands on the back of his pants, extended his right in belated introduction, but turned it up just before hers met it and studied the grease, then shrugged and let it fall to his side. His gaze took in her own immaculate appearance, skimming the soft blouse and fitted jeans beneath her open hip-length parka and resting momentarily on the toes of her fine leather boots before returning to her face. "Sorry about that. Wouldn't want to get you dirty."

"No problem," she countered quickly, anxious to get down to business. "That *was* your work I saw this morning, wasn't it?"

"It was." He cocked his hands on his hips.

"It's impressive," she ventured. But when he held her gaze unwaveringly, without any sign of appreciation, she forced herself on. "I've bought a house just outside of town and want some work done on it. It's a large job, but you'd be well compensated." At his look of mild disinterest, she added cautiously, "You *are* available, aren't you?"

"No."

Taken aback by his abruptness, she frowned. "No? That's strange. I was told that you were just finishing a job. In fact, Mr. O'Hara went out of his way to tell me that he was sure you'd be able to help me."

The amber eyes narrowed. "O'Hara, was it?" He grimaced and looked away, focusing on a distant mountain top. "O'Hara's a crafty one," he murmured more softly, then returned his full attention to Debra. "But

9

I'm afraid I can't help you." Turning, he bent to retrieve the wrench he'd dropped beneath the truck, leaving Debra nothing but the broad expanse of his back to study. She wasn't about to be satisfied with that alone.

"Then . . . you have another job lined up?"

"Nope." Wrench in hand, he straightened and crossed the garage to replace the tool on its hook. Debra followed.

"I don't understand. If you're finishing one job and don't have another in the offing, why won't you consider mine?"

Digging into the pocket of his shirt, he withdrew the broken stub of a pencil, looked at it in disgust before tossing it aside, then began to search the open shelves for one that was in better condition. Debra's question hung in the air while the shuffle of nails and screws went on until he found what he wanted. Tearing a sheet of paper from a grimy pad, he covered it with a broad scrawl.

"Here are a couple of names. Either of these men should be able to help. And they need the work far more than I do."

"But it's your work I want," she protested, finding the sheet thrust in her hand nonetheless as Graham stalked off toward a soft-drink machine, fished in his pocket for change and came up empty-handed. Within seconds, she produced the coins he needed and threaded them into the slot. "What'll it be?"

He hesitated for just a moment. "Mountain Dew. I'll owe you."

"Forget it. Call it a consultation fee." Determined, she pulled hard on the knob, waited for the can to drop, then boldly handed it to the man beside her.

He held it briefly, wavering, thirstily anticipating the cool contents of the can. Yet one part of him didn't want anything from a woman wearing designer jeans and imported boots, particularly as strong-minded a woman as this one appeared to be.

Unfortunately, though, while strong-minded meant trouble, it also intrigued him. When his finger found the ring at the top of the can and drew it back, letting loose a gentle hiss, he couldn't help but feel it was Pandora's box he'd knowingly opened.

"Can we talk?" she asked again, glancing around for a suitable spot, looking back in time to see the carpenter take a deep swig of the drink. His throat was strong, its muscles channeling both the liquid and her gaze lower, down a path of hair-roughened skin past one empty buttonhole to one not so, where she was forced to let the fluid continue alone. Stunned by her fascination with the raw strength he exuded, she quickly averted her eyes to study the quiet cluster of buildings just beyond, on the town's main street. "Is there a restaurant nearby?" she asked softly. "It's been a while since breakfast."

Graham's lips twitched at one corner. "I'm not exactly dressed for dining," he noted with wry exaggeration of the words.

Debra was undaunted by his mockery. "I wasn't thinking of the Ritz," she quipped. "Surely there's a sandwich shop that wouldn't be offended by the sight of grease."

"*You*'re not?" A tawny brow arched under the hair that now fell to cover his forehead.

"Of course not," she chided. "Well? Is there somewhere we can go? Or are *you* embarrassed to be seen?"

Absently, he raised a hand to rub his jaw, realized he was simply spreading the grime around and held the offending fingers out to the side. His grin was a sheepish one. "That bad, huh?"

"I don't mind," Debra drawled indulgently, rather enjoying the sheer physicality of the man. Such a harmless issue, dirt.

But there was something else at stake. Graham eyed her more sharply, all hint of humor gone. He drew himself up straighter and spoke more coolly. "Look, there's really no point to our talking. I can't work for you. It's as simple as that."

She refused to accept it. "You don't even know what the job entails. How can you blindly refuse it?" Raising the soda to his lips, he took a leisurely swallow. In his own time, he spoke. "I'm self-employed. I can accept or reject jobs as I choose." When he turned and stalked toward his truck, she kept pace.

"Please, Mr. Reid. I don't quite know why you won't hear me out, but I do know that you'd be the best man to do my job." Running ahead, she flattened herself against the door of the truck in a measure of sheer desperation. Having seen samples of his work and knowing now what she'd miss, she couldn't simply let him drive away.

Standing back, he dropped his eyes to the paper she still held in her hand. "Forbes or Campbell will do fine. Either one. Give them a call."

"But I've seen their work," she persisted calmly, straightening her shoulders and holding her chin steady. "Yours is better."

The amber eyes bore into her. "Flattery will get you nowhere, Miss—"

"Barry. Debra Barry." Out of habit, she extended her hand, only then recalling his earlier thwarted attempt at the same. When he scowled, she buried the hand in her pocket. "And I'm not trying to flatter you. I'm simply stating the truth. I've spent the entire morning driving the local roads, studying the renovation work that's been done here lately. Yours is consistently the most exciting. You're the man I want."

Staring down at her, Graham had to admire her spunk. She wasn't tall; the heels of her boots gave her an edge that, flat-footed, she wouldn't have. Nor was she heavy. Even the bulk of her parka couldn't hide the slimness of her body. And then there was the gentleness of her features. But features could be deceptive, he reminded himself as he helplessly endured the chill that shot through him.

Upending the soda can at his lips, he drained its contents, crushed the can one-handed and lobbed it into a nearby barrel. Then, reaching for the coat he'd discarded earlier, he hauled it from where it lay across the side edge of the pickup and thrust his arms into its sleeves. "What *did* you have in mind," he heard himself ask as he straightened the collar. When the face before him brightened, he instantly regretted raising her hopes. But the deed had been done. And, as he suspected, Debra Barry wasted no time spicing up the lure.

"Everything." Her eyes glowed in sudden excitement. "I want the house totally renovated."

"Where is the place?"

She cocked her head westward. "It's off Woodbury, about a mile from the center of town, just beyond the lake . . . ?"

"The only place for sale in that direction is the Richardson house." He eyed her more cautiously and with a touch of disbelief. "You've bought the old Richardson house?"

"That's right," she answered with pride.

"That's just about the oldest house in the county! It's been neglected for years. I'm not sure whether *any* of it is salvageable."

"That's where you come in."

His large hand came up, lean fingers straight. "Now just a minute. I haven't agreed to do anything."

"But you want to hear more, don't you?" she coaxed, betting on the hunch that a man who had planned and executed the work she'd seen that morning wouldn't be able to pass up a challenge such as the one she offered.

His gaze narrowed on the warm humor in her eyes, which were brown like her hair, he suddenly realized. Neither was striking, yet both gleamed. Had his hands not been so filthy, he might have been tempted to touch the tendril of smooth silk that had fallen from the sophisticated twist low on her nape and now brushed her cheek. Instead, he cleared his throat and reached past her to the door handle. "Excuse me."

Debra's face sobered instantly. "I've lost? But *why?*" She moved aside as Graham pulled the cab door open. Then he half-turned and gestured toward the seats.

"I've decided I'm hungry, after all." He sounded bored. "I'd help you up, but you're really too clean to touch." Eyes on a sleek sports car that sped down the street en route to a more plush destination, he awaited her decision, all the while struggling with his own second thoughts.

She didn't leave him time to think. Her hopes alive once more, she climbed up and slid behind the steering wheel to the passenger's side before he could change his mind. By the time he had settled beside her, she had readied her second plan of attack.

"It's a terrific house," she began, her eyes never leaving him as he started the engine and backed the truck from the bay, turned it and headed onto the main street. "Historically, it's a gem."

"I know" was the terse reply.

She studied his face, its rugged outline dramatized by the smudge of dirt on his jaw. "What *do* you know?" she asked on impulse.

"About the Richardson house?" He shot her a fast glance as he slowed to allow for a car entering the road ahead. "Not that much more than O'Hara told you, I suspect." He shrugged. "It was built over two hundred years ago by a shipwright who died in the Revolutionary War. His descendants lived there until the start of this century, but its ownership has turned over too many times to count since then. It simply got too run-down and required too much money to make it comfortable." With a deft twist of his arm, he turned the wheel and guided the truck onto a side street lined with bare-armed trees.

"But it's got potential, wouldn't you say, Mr. Reid?"

His jaw tensed. "It's Graham. And yes. It does have potential."

As Debra wondered at his grudging admission, he pulled into a free spot before a small building, one of several on the quiet street. "I'll go ahead in and use the washroom. Why don't you find us a seat," he commanded. Before she could respond, he'd slid from the truck and shut the door behind him.

Startled, she watched as he loped up the path to the door of the restaurant and disappeared. Strange man, she mused. Compelling in his way—certainly talented from the looks of the work she'd seen, but strange. Eyes clouded in bemusement, she helped herself from the truck, and pulling her coat more snugly against the early April chill, headed for the door through which he'd gone.

What on the outside had been a simple structure was no less unpretentious inside. Debra found herself in a room dotted with round, bare tables, about half of which were occupied by a collection of casually dressed men and an even smaller number of women. A far cry from her usual luncheon spots, she reflected as she headed for a free table in a quiet corner. Once seated, she propped her arms on those of an old oak chair and waited for her carpenter to return.

For he *was* her carpenter, she vowed, whether he was ready to admit it or not. She knew his weak spot. She'd found it in the skill of the work she'd seen that morning, in his knowledge of design and attention to detail. Had these not given him away, the glowing recommendations of those he'd worked for would have. Dedicated. Serious. Innovative. Brilliant. Pleasant. Pleasant? Recalling the way he'd grinned once or twice, albeit seemingly against his will, she saw the potential in him. Perhaps beneath that layer of wariness, beneath that sheath of toughness and muscle, *was* somewhere hidden a pleasant man.

Graham's expression was far from pleasant, however, when he emerged several minutes later from the back room. The time he'd spent washing had been time spent in ardent self-reproach for having allowed this woman to con him into having lunch with her. Oh, yes, he'd been the one who'd finally made the move, but it had been her wiliness that had driven him to it. In her own gently persistent way, she was dangerous, he mused, frowning as he scanned the room to find her sitting, quietly awaiting him. Her eyes met his instantly and followed him as he crossed the room. By the time he reached the table, he was all the more resolute.

"I can't take your job, Miss Barry."

"Debra."

He pulled out a chair and eased into it, careful to keep himself a fair distance from her. "Whatever—"

"No, it's Debra." She repressed a smile. "I get violent when people call me 'whatever.'"

He paused, shifting gears. "Does it happen often?" he rejoined, quite without intending to, yet somehow lured by her lighthearted air.

"No. It's really 'darling' or 'sweetie' that gets my goat more often," she mused aloud, thinking of that world from which she'd come.

Filing the information, Graham grew more curious. "Do you get violent often?"

Debra grinned. "If you're asking whether I'll be easy to work for, I can assure you—"

That momentarily sobered him. "I'm not working for you."

"I see." She lowered her head and studied the menu. "Any recommendations?"

"I gave you two. You haven't lost the paper already, have you?"

"For lunch." She pertly corrected his misinterpretation. "Is there anything I should try?"

Swinging again with her humor, Graham made a pretense of deep thought. Then he sighed. "There's a great grilled cheese here. Or you could have a hot dog. They boil 'em just so. On the other hand, the egg salad is served on French bread. That's exciting . . . if it's fresh."

"Now you're mocking me . . . or them," she chided just softly enough to take his notice. "But I'm serious. You must eat here a lot. What do you suggest?"

"For the record," he returned, "I rarely eat here. When I'm on a job, I eat at the site."

"Which brings us back to my proposal. And your refusal of it. If you're just about to finish one job, why won't you consider doing mine next?"

"Beef stew."

She frowned. "What?"

"Try the beef stew. It's served with warm cornbread. Very good."

As frustration vied with amusement for supremacy in her thoughts, Debra could only stare silently at this enigmatic carpenter. His face was now clean, and she contrasted the roughness of his cheek with the smoothness of the bone at its crown. The faint crow's-feet at the corners of his eyes attested to the sense of humor she'd just sampled. The furrows on his brow, revealed beneath newly combed hair, correspondingly spoke of his more serious side. He was a puzzlement, she decided. Or was he simply leery of newcomers, as some of those others she'd met had been? They were wary, these granite state denizens, of city folk. She half-agreed with them.

"Beef stew it will be," she announced, closing her menu and dropping it flat. Then, intertwining her fingers on the table, she forged ahead. "What I want is a total renovation of the house. It needs new electrical, plumbing and heating systems. I assume you'll want to contract those out."

"I'm not taking the job," Graham reiterated, though he sat back in his seat and listened to her every word.

Debra shrugged at the irrelevancy of his protest, then went on as though he'd said nothing. "The excitement comes in the structural changes I've got planned."

"You've got planned? Are you an architect?"

She grinned and shook her head, her gaze narrowing. "If only I were, I wouldn't have to be so concerned about the man I hire to do the job. No"—she sighed—"I've got no degree, just lots of ideas of my own. The problem is that I don't know whether they'll be practical . . . or feasible." She took a breath. "That's one of the things you'll need to tell me."

In a silent bid for patience, Graham looked skyward. When he lowered his gaze once more, it held a benign indulgence. "I don't *need* to tell you anything, lady," he drawled.

"Debra. It's Debra. 'Lady' sounds too much like a dog."

Leaning suddenly closer, he put his forearms on the table. His face was dangerously near. "Debra, you're barking up the wrong tree." He sat back as quickly as he'd lunged forward, allowing her to release the breath she'd unknowingly caught. "Besides, from the sounds of it, you ought to demolish the place and start from scratch. If you're so displeased with it as it is—"

"But I'm not!" she exclaimed. "I love it. The setting

is perfect; so is the basic outer design of the house. Sure, it will take time and effort to make it livable. But it will be worth it."

"Will it?" he asked indifferently. Twisting his head, he motioned to the waitress and called their orders to her before turning back to Debra. "It'll cost you a bundle."

"I know."

"And you've got it?"

"What kind of a question is that? Do you always ask prospective employers about their finances?"

A faint smile slanted his lips, lending him a roguish air that melted her feeble indignation. "Only when I feel they may not have any idea what the job will entail."

"Then you *will* consider taking it?"

The smile vanished. "No."

"Damn it, Graham." She sat forward, her eyes pleading. "Why *not?*"

"Because it'll take too long, for one thing. I've seen that house. Even studied it. You're right. The design is great. And I can almost begin to imagine some of the things you've got in mind. Certain things—like that sloped-roof addition—just beg for skylights over a paneled den—"

"Study. It's going to be a study, with yards of desk space, a comfortable telephone extension, several easy chairs and a ceiling filled with natural light. I'm not sure whether I want a raised-dome or a flat-panel skylight, though. And as for double-glazed versus triple-glazed glass—"

"As long as you avoid plastic, either one is fine. Triple glazed is great if you can get it. But it would have to be special ordered. There may be a wait."

Debra smiled. "I'm in no rush. That's the beauty of it. As long as I have a corner in which to live during the work, you can take all the time you want."

"I don't want to take *any* time," Graham reminded her archly.

She gave a grandiose nod. "That's right. I keep forgetting. Ah!" She looked up. "Here comes the stew. It had better be good if I'm going to be able to believe any of your recommendations."

The carpenter was far less bothered by her humor than he would have liked. By rights, he should have found her persistence irksome. By rights, he should have found *her* irksome. But he didn't. Rather, he found something sweet in her humor, just as he'd earlier admired that gentleness in her features. It had been a long time since he'd engaged in such crisp banter. Unfortunately, he enjoyed it.

As she smiled her thanks to the waitress, he watched her turn her attention to the beef stew, and he knew that he'd have to find something bothersome about her—quickly.

"Well?" he asked, awaiting her verdict on the food. It had to be a far cry from the boeuf bourgignon she may have expected. If he was lucky, she'd hate it.

Tipping her head sideways, she finished a sample mouthful. "Not bad. Not bad at all. I may just let you special order those triple-glazed skylights."

The mischievous gleam in her eye did nothing for Graham's peace of mind. Turning on his own stew, he attacked it vengefully. It was only Debra's soft voice moments later that broke into his turmoil.

"Graham, why won't you take the job?" There was no humor in her voice now, simply the quiet need to know. She'd fallen in love with his work as quickly as she'd fallen in love with the old decaying house she'd bought in one fast day. "From what I've seen, you do both modern work and restorations. My job would entail both." When his dark head remained bowed and he continued to eat, she took another bite, then set down her spoon. "I really need your help. I want this house to be perfect."

Graham slowly looked up. "Why? Why does it mean that much to you? After all, it's just a house."

"It's *my* house," she retorted more sharply than she'd intended, then quickly gentled her voice. But she had his full attention. "It's mine. Something of my own, for the first time in my life. Now that may mean nothing to you. I have no idea where you've come from in life. But being a working man, I would have assumed you'd understand. Furthermore, you're a carpenter. Surely you can see the physical, if not the emotional, value of that house. But there's no point in making *any* investment in the place if I don't do it right." She paused to study his staid expression. "Am I getting through at all?" she asked hesitantly.

"On the last . . . yes. I agree with you there. If you've got the means to do it, that house could be spectacular. And I do understand what it means to actually own something. . . ."

His voice trailed off as his mind took another turn. She'd spoken of owning the house herself, of needing the smallest corner in which to live. The implication was that she'd be alone. That *would* be tempting the devil. On the other hand, if he'd misinterpreted her words and she'd have someone with her—a husband, or lover. No, that would be worse. He'd be nothing more than a Peeping Tom. But what about a relative?

"Tell me," he began speculatively.

"Anything!" she exclaimed with such enthusiasm that he held up a hand to curb it.

"Easy, woman."

"Debra. It's Debra."

"Don't like 'woman,' either?" He shot her a heavy-lidded glance. "See? We'd never make it spending all that time together."

Ignoring his quip, she jumped ahead. "How much time do you think it will take?"

"I couldn't tell you that without examining the place in detail, drawing up plans and working through specifications. It's April now. If the work is begun within the next few weeks, you've a good chance of having it done by fall."

Her eyes widened. "That long? I assumed that with crews working on different parts simultaneously, it'd be faster."

Graham lowered his head and glared at her mockingly. "That may be true in the big city, love. But this is the country. Sure, there are different crews. Even someone like me who prefers to work alone calls in specialists for the mechanical systems."

"Mechanical systems?"

"Plumbing, heating—that type of thing. But that's where the delays can begin. In an area like this, there are only so many specialists available. Like you, I'd want the best. And the best may live two hours away and may not be free precisely when you need him. Then there are snags in deliveries. For example, a house like the Richardson place should be shingled. I'm not talking about cheap stuff. Cedar shingles are the best, and the ones I have in mind aren't always in ready supply. Am I getting through at all?" he asked in echo of her earlier words.

"I hear you," she answered softly, then looked away in disappointment. "And I really am in no rush. But I kind of thought I'd be living in style by August."

Words she'd chosen quite lightly struck her companion as quite the opposite. Living in style? Perhaps she should have stayed in the city. "Exactly what is it you're looking for, Debra?" he asked in quiet demand.

She tipped her chin higher. "A home."

"All by yourself?" He finally got the question out.

"You haven't mentioned anyone else. Is there someone you'll be living with?"

After a brief pause, she shook her head. "No." Her voice dropped in mock confidence. "But don't go spreading the word, will you? I'd rather not publicize a thing like that."

"You'll be safe," he stated coldly. Debra looked up, but his expression was masked, his mind set simply on his finishing his lunch. She watched him nonetheless, noting that there was nothing of the backwoods handyman in the way he ate. Indeed, had the setting been a trendy café in New York, he would have fit in. There was something about him, something of a worldliness beneath the rough veneer. It came through in his work as well.

When at last he was done, she broached the subject a final time. "Graham," she began in her most convincing voice, having no way of knowing that the tone would harden him all the more, "I really want you to do my house."

Sitting back in his chair with his elbows propped comfortably on its stubby wooden arms, he linked his fingers together in a show of nonchalance that belied the disquiet of his gaze. "I'm sorry" was all he said.

"Reasons," she persisted. "At least if I'm being refused flat out, I have a right to know the reasons behind the refusal."

"The job's too large."

"Baloney! You mentioned that before, and it doesn't hold water. You said that you've got nothing lined up." A thought hit. "You're not leaving the area, are you?"

"No."

"Then what's the problem? If I'm willing to pay, how can you possibly refuse a job that will guarantee you employment for four or five months."

"Six or seven. But it's not a matter of money."

"Of course it's not," she came back. "My offer is a beauty from a professional standpoint alone. How can you pass up the chance to redo a house like that, soup to nuts, with free rein to do what you want?"

He slanted her a cynical smile. "Free rein? Weren't you the one who spoke of the plans *you* had?"

"Well . . . yes . . ." she waffled, then raced on. "But everything's up for discussion. There's so much I don't know. I don't even *know* what I don't know."

"What in the hell does that mean?"

"It means that you could make suggestions I've never dreamed of and I might love them. Think of what I might miss if you refuse me."

"But then," he pointed out darkly, "you'll never *know* what you've missed, will you?"

She sat straighter and frowned. "Have I done something to offend you?"

"Why do you ask that?"

"Because I get the distinct impression that your refusal is a personal one. There's something about me that annoys you, isn't there?" Without awaiting an answer, she barreled on. "Tell me one thing, Graham. If I had called you on the phone—better still, if my husband had called . . ." The words died in her throat when she realized what she'd said. It had been a natural slip. The ink had barely dried on the divorce decree. Blinking against a flicker of pain, she cleared her throat. "If you'd gotten a blind phone call describing this very job, would you have refused it then and there, or would you have made an appointment with the buyer to look through the house?"

Deep in thought, Graham stared at her. When his gaze darted momentarily to her left hand, she stifled the urge to hide it in her lap. It still felt naked without the ring it had worn for so long.

"You're separated?" he asked quietly.

24

Though she would rather not have had this discussion arise, Debra saw no point in evasion. "Divorced."

"Recently?"

"Yes."

He nodded, his hair falling on his brow, lessening the impact of his glower. She was divorced, living alone, available. And if he'd correctly read that shimmer of pain, she was vulnerable. It would be all too easy to take advantage of her. Though she was a city girl and, as such, poison for him, he was human. The demands of rural living and the closeness of working together, should he take the job, would be trying. Already he could imagine the frustration he might feel. There was something uncomfortably appealing about her.

He thrust his fingers through his hair in a gesture of irritation. Then he looked her in the eye. "Yes, it's personal. I have this thing against wealthy women who toy with life in the backwoods."

Startled, she clenched her fist. "I'm not asking you to marry me, for God's sake! I'm simply asking you to do some work on my house!" Looking out the window, she threw her hand in the air and let it fall with a slap on the hard wood of the table. "I don't believe this," she murmured in disbelief, then looked sharply back at him. "I mean, I assumed you people would be somewhat . . . parochial . . . but I had hoped for common sense. For your information, I'm neither a 'wealthy' woman nor one who is 'toying with life in the backwoods.' I'll be pouring every last cent I have into this house, . . . and I have no intention of *ever* returning to the city! Now if that's 'toying with life in the backwoods,' then you're not as bright as I'd thought." Furious, she shoved her arms into the sleeves of her coat, which had cushioned her on the chair, reached for her purse and withdrew a bill from her wallet. "Here. My share." She'd barely thrust the money at him when he caught her wrist and held it firmly.

"It's on me," he growled, as aware as she of the fire between them. "I'm a bit past the Dutch-treat stage, and I can't stand a liberated woman."

"I thought you didn't have any money," she snapped, helpless to free herself from his burning grip.

"I have money." In slow motion, he released her hand, then reached to his back pocket. "No change. But I do have money."

"Then I'll owe you—less the cost of one Mountain Dew." Rising in a burst of frustration, she turned and left the restaurant, finding peace in the quiet, overcast afternoon air only until she realized that she'd need a lift back to the service station to retrieve her rental car. As she leaned back sheepishly against the door of the truck, her anger slowly began to subside. She barely had time to wonder at its force when the very cause of her annoyance casually emerged from the restaurant and approached, looking eminently masculine and thoroughly self-contained.

"Need a lift?"

"You know I do. If it wouldn't be too much trouble. I can see how busy you are."

"Now, now," he chided, smiling wickedly, "no need for sarcasm. Just because you're not used to being turned down . . ."

"It's got nothing to do with that! I don't mind losing if the reasons are just. Yours aren't!"

Graham stretched an arm over her shoulder to grasp the door handle, but he left her no room to move aside. He was dangerously close, frighteningly large. For a split second, Debra wondered if it was for the best that he wouldn't accept her job. He was a totally different kind of man than any she'd ever known—physical rather than cerebral. He was a threat . . . and an enticement. Damn it, though, she loved his work . . .

"Look, Debra," he began, his voice deep and guarded. "You know nothing about me."

"I've seen your work."

"I don't like New York women."

She forced a harsh laugh. "Now that's even *more* bigoted. And what makes you so sure I'm from New York?"

"Your speech, for one thing. There's a distinct sound to words when spoken by a native New Yorker. I'd guess you've spent time elsewhere, but you've always returned to the city."

She tried to ignore the discrepancy in their height, but her head was bent back against the truck as she looked up. "I could be from upstate New York."

"Uh-uh. It's too strong. But then there are other things, like your makeup and your hair."

Reflexively, she touched the knot at the nape of her neck. "What's wrong with my hair . . . or my makeup, for that matter?"

"Nothing," he admitted dispassionately. "They're perfect."

"And that's it, isn't it?"

He nodded slowly. "You even smell of Manhattan. What's that—Magie Noir, Chanel?"

"It's Lauren. And it happens that I saw it on sale at a drugstore here this morning."

"Did you happen to notice the dust on the top of the box?" he asked, then continued as his meaning set in. "But even beyond that, it's the way you're dressed." His gaze hung on her lips for a minute before slipping down to admire her blouse and jeans. She felt his amber warmth at every stop. "It's country chic for city dwellers. Come to think of it, I'm sure I saw an outfit similar to that from Saks, maybe Bloomingdale's, in last Sunday's paper."

He had all the answers, and Debra felt suddenly tired. She couldn't seem to win with men lately, and she just wasn't up for prolonging the fight. Besides, there was something about this man, something about the way his body sheltered hers, that drove all thought of fight from mind. And *that* thought was immensely unsettling.

"Okay," she said, admitting quiet defeat as she stared at the textured hollow of his throat. "You win. I refuse to apologize for who I am and where I'm from. If you'd just be so kind as to return me to my car, I'll be on my way."

When he didn't move, she looked up in surprise. His gaze burned into her, much as his fingers had done on that one occasion they'd touched her wrist. It was as though there was a glowing world within him, one that threatened—and beckoned—even more than the raw carnality of the carpenter he was on the surface.

Then he pulled himself straight with a slow indrawn breath and moved back to give her room before opening the door. He saw her safely seated before he shut the door and rounded the truck to the driver's side.

Neither spoke as he retraced their earlier route. But when he pulled up at the curb of the service station, his voice came through loud and clear, deep and firm. "If I've offended you, I'm sorry. It's me, really. There's nothing wrong with who and what you are . . . other than that I'd have trouble working with you." His eyes never left the windshield, nor his hands the wheel. She could see the whiteness of his knuckles and wondered again at that other world within. But it wasn't her concern.

"I appreciate your honesty," she spoke quietly. "Not that it makes it any easier. I'm still convinced that you'd be the best man for the job *and* that you'd be able to do it completely forgetting my presence. After all," she scoffed softly, "I wouldn't be looking over your shoulder or anything. What do *I* know of construction? And besides, I have my own work to do." With a tug at the handle, the door opened. She slid from the truck with all the dignity she could muster, turning only at the last to enter a final plea. To her relief, he met her gaze. "If you should change your mind and want to take a look at the place, I'll be there from late this afternoon on."

His eyes darkened. "You're living there? But there can't be any heat!"

She smiled at his concern until she realized that it was nothing more than chauvinistic disbelief, and the smile vanished. "There's a fireplace and plenty of wood. And I've just bought the heaviest sleeping bag in the county. We city girls aren't as fragile as you country boys would like to believe," she ended sweetly. "Thanks for the lunch."

With a bang, she closed the door and walked to her car without looking back. She was well on the road before the man behind the wheel of the truck revved his motor, shoved the gear shift into drive and took off.

It was late the following morning when he arrived at the Richardson house.

Chapter Two

*H*aving spent the better part of the night debating the wisdom of his even considering the job, Graham was as surprised as Debra to find himself on her doorstep. It was the challenge, he told himself, the irresistible lure of designing and building. He hadn't yet come up with an explanation for his having shaved and showered with special care, much less for having laid out slacks and a sweater before rejecting them in favor of clean jeans and a shirt. Here he was a carpenter; he'd have to remember that. Nor had he been able to justify his having totally sacrificed a day of work other than to reason that he owed himself the time.

Debra didn't recognize the truck at first. She'd been so engrossed in her work that it had been nearly upon her before its sound penetrated her concentration. Jumping from her makeshift desk, she stared out the window at the dark brown pickup that had come to a halt behind her car on the graveled drive. The midday sun, wending its steadfast way through the branches of the oak, as it would never be able to do come May, bounced radiantly off both shiny hoods.

Opening the door on a wave of cautious pleasure, she smiled. "Ah, I see you've washed the truck . . . *and* you," she observed, content to attribute the rapid beat of her heart to the apparent salvation of the house. Her night had been no more restful than his, and she had concluded that he was probably right. It wouldn't work. They'd have to coexist too closely. If he had reservations, regardless of their merit, it boded ill for the entire project.

She asked herself why he was here, then . . . and why he looked so good. A carpenter was supposed to be rugged and earthy, not fresh and refined. And while she suddenly wished she hadn't pressed him, it was too late for those second thoughts. He was here. And from the look on his face, he was all business. That was some solace.

"I thought I'd take a walk around," he ventured in an even tone, casting a glance over her shoulder to the burning fire, the cluster of suitcases by the wall, the array of notebooks and papers on a large board bridging two cinder blocks. "Am I disturbing you?"

"No, no!" Not knowing what to do with her hands, she anchored them in the back pockets of her jeans. Today they were faded ones, topped by an old Columbia sweatshirt. In sneakers, she was indeed much shorter. "I was, uh, working."

"Working?" Following the trend of her thoughts, he stared at her outfit. A switch, he had to admit. Even her hair was less formal, caught above one ear by a thin ribbon and falling in a pony tail to her shoulder. "Cleaning up?"

When she shook her head, the pony tail swished gently. "I did that yesterday . . . what little I intend to do, that is. There's not much sense doing a whole lot if the place is going to be torn up pretty soon."

"I can't believe you're actually living here."

She eyed him in quiet defiance. "That's what you said yesterday. But why not? I've a roof over my head, a fire in the hearth, an ancient stove in an ancient kitchen. They've even turned on the electricity for me—what more could a woman ask?"

"She usually asks for luxury. Weren't you the one bemoaning the fact that this job could take as long as six or seven months?"

"That was disappointment you heard, not disgust. There's a difference. Not that I'm knocking luxury, mind you. When I'm finished with this house, it will be exquisite. But I can live without for a while." She grinned shyly, leaning back against the crusty doorknob. "Besides, I really have no choice. I haven't anyone around here to stay with. And I can't bear the thought of living in a motel. This will be fine."

The look Graham cast her held its share of doubt. She seemed far too fragile to be roughing it in an old, drafty house. But then, he mused, that was her choice. He'd simply come to look around, to poke at a few boards, to take some measurements. If he took the job—and a big *if* it remained—he wouldn't be her keeper.

Reminded of his purpose, he patted the outer flaps of his windbreaker, then the pockets of his jeans. Then he turned abruptly. "I'll be right back." Within minutes, he returned with a folding tape measure, a notebook and a pencil. Debra hadn't moved. "You *will* let me in, won't you?" he asked, puzzled by her immobility in the doorway. Then he breathed in and tensed. "Or is the job filled?"

Instantly, she stepped back. "No! It's not filled. I wasn't going to give up on you until this afternoon. Then I would have had to go after one of the others. But I'm glad you've come."

He arched a brow. Following its direction, she noted that, clean, his hair was less brown and more tawny. It was thick and easily hit the top of his collar in back, longer than the current city style. Refreshing.

His voice cut into her thoughts. "I'm not promising anything," he cautioned. He hadn't yet stepped over the threshold. "I may find it more than I want."

Belatedly aware of the unintended double meaning of his words, he quickly went on. "But you're right. For an—for a builder, this is too much of a temptation. I feel I owe it to myself at least to take a look."

Debra gave him her most innocent smile. "No excuses, please." And a genuine welcome. "I'm just grateful you're here." She gestured toward the living room. "Come on in."

He *hadn't* yet stepped over the threshold. That knowledge was mildly reassuring. "Uh, let me start out here. I'd like to see what has to be done structurally, what needs to be repaired." Backing up, he left the walk and crossed the dry grass to study the exterior of the house.

Debra followed him, closing the door behind to keep in the warmth supplied by the fire. She'd need an entirely new heating system; but then *he'd* know that without having to spend a night in the cold as she'd done. It hadn't been that bad, she told herself. Her sleeping bag had been toasty, and within the week her bed would arrive, along with more of her things. An electric blanket would do wonders until the air warmed up. And, miraculously, there had been plenty of hot water for a bath. No, it hadn't been that bad. Kind of exciting in a romantic sort of way. As a city girl, she'd always wondered . . .

"When did you assume ownership?" Graham asked, his eyes glued to the worn shingles as though willing them to stay in place.

She came close and helped him stare at the shingles. "Two days ago."

"Had you been looking at it long?"

"No. But I knew the general area in which I wanted to live and the type of place I wanted. When I saw this, I knew I'd struck pay dirt."

He chuckled. "Pay dirt may strike *you* by the time you finish doing what has to be done. See that frame?"

She followed the straight line of his finger to one of the second-floor windows. "Can you see the distortion, particularly on the left?"

"Uh-huh."

"Something isn't providing the support it should. There may be moisture seeping into those walls. When I go in, I'll take a look. It could be that dampness is collecting under the eaves. And that's another thing."

"I need a new roof."

"Right. Assuming the support underneath is solid, that's not such a huge problem. And if you want skylights put in, there'd be a lot of cutting, anyway."

Liking both his knowledge and his enthusiasm, Debra smiled to herself. He might easily be able to resist her, but it was very possible that he'd never be able to resist her house. There was hope yet. Wrapping her arms around herself to ward off the chill, she gave him a sidelong glance. "What about working in some kind of solar heating system? Is it feasible?"

His eye scanned the roof, the overhanging trees, the position of the sun. "I'll have to see the back. You run in and get a coat while I make some notes here first."

"I'm fine."

"You're cold. Go on." He cast her a punishing glance. "You won't miss anything."

Reluctant to argue when she felt she'd begun to smell victory, Debra returned to the house for her parka, draped it over her shoulders and rejoined him. His pencil moved rapidly over the page of his notebook, pausing now and again when he looked up in renewed study.

She watched him, admiring the way he stood, then walked with a kind of feral grace toward the house to finger the worn siding. Wandering across the yard, she settled down atop one of the more sturdy sections of the ragged split-rail fence and turned her admiration full force on her house.

It was most simply a two-story wood-frame house with a steeply pitched attic above whose high peak rose a central brick chimney. The design had become truly interesting because of additions that had been built over the years—the lean-to tacked onto the left side, with a smaller chimney of its own, the servants' rooms built onto the rear, the small carriage house connected on the right by a trellised breezeway.

Sitting back in silent appreciation, Debra once more basked in a kind of down-home warmth exuded by the house. It was from another era, one that had to have been simpler, she mused, allowing herself to recall New York only briefly before checking her watch. It was not yet noon. She had another ninety minutes. Surely Graham wouldn't be here that long.

Turning her attention to him once more, she found him returning the favor. "I'm sorry!" She jumped up. "Did you want me?"

Swallowing a bitter laugh, he shook his head and started slowly around the house. By all means, he wanted her. Wasn't that half the problem? As he'd stood there looking at her, he'd felt a surge of desire the likes of which he hadn't felt in years. For all her talk of having found precisely what she wanted, at times—fleeting seconds—she seemed lost. Small, alone, lost. Or was that wishful thinking on his part?

Plodding more angrily toward the back of the house, he listened to the rustle underfoot of leaves long dead. When he stopped to examine what looked to be rotted wood at the base of the wall, he heard the echo of steps behind him.

"Several of these wall sills may need to be replaced," he said without turning. "See this?" He jabbed at one with the end of his pencil and easily broke off several large splinters. "It's probably an original." He squinted up toward the roof. "A lot of this has been replaced at least once. That roof may be the third or fourth. And each time the quality of the new material gets worse."

She'd come up on his right to observe his demonstration. "Yesterday you talked of cedar shingles. Is that what you'd recommend?"

"They'd sure as hell beat those asphalt things that have been slapped up. You couldn't go far wrong doing both the roof *and* the side walls with cedar. The best ones are pretreated with a fire retardant. They weather so beautifully that you don't even have to stain them. And that's another worry to be free of down the road a bit." He paused to send her a piercing glance. "Are you planning to stay that long?"

"I'm planning to *live* here. I mean, obviously, if I'm run over by a truck next month, I won't be here that long."

"What a gruesome sense of humor you have," he grumbled. "You know what I meant."

"You meant to ask when I'd tire of 'toying with life in the backwoods.' How can I convince you that I'm here to stay?"

His amber gaze was pointed. "Why?"

"Why am I here to stay?" she asked. At his single nod, she shrugged, drawing on the safest of her many reasons for having come. "I've always wanted to live in the country. What better place than this? I've also always wanted to design my own home."

"Then why not buy a piece of land and build a new house rather than doctoring up this relic? It'd be a lot easier in some respects."

She tipped her head pertly to the side. "But not half the fun. And besides, there's something about continuity . . ." She struggled for the words to express her thoughts. "Something about feeling roots, if not to one's own past, then to that of others. You said it yourself—this is one of the oldest houses around. I like that."

Her answer had ended on such an up note that Graham couldn't even fault its simplicity. "I'll tell you something else you'll like," he said, starting to walk again, this time toward the back yard, his eyes all the while on the house. "The foundation looks good. I can't see signs of buckling. Sometimes with the settling of a house over the years, you run into trouble. I think you're okay, though I'd have to take a look inside."

"Will you?" she asked hopefully.

He dropped his chin to his chest, looked sideways at her, then refocused on the rear wall of the house. "Not yet," he said with such firmness that she didn't dare push. Putting pencil to paper, he resumed his note taking, approaching the house to prod one point or another, stepping back to look up before moving on.

Giving him room, Debra strolled farther into the yard, heading toward a weathered wooden love seat that swung from the sturdy arm of a chestnut tree. She'd turned and half-lowered herself when Graham's bark brought her instantly upright.

"Is that safe?"

"Sure, it's safe."

"How do you know?"

"Because I sat in it the day I first looked at the house, and after the way the realtor warned me about every stone that was out of place on the walk, I'm sure he'd never have let me sit on the swing if he'd had any doubt that it would hold. He wouldn't want a lawsuit on his hands. Besides"—she grinned—"he had this humongous dog with him. We let the dog test it out."

She barely heard a deep "Hmmmmph" before Graham returned to his inspection. Settling comfortably on the seat, she swung it gently, finding the rhythmic moan of the rusted metalwork to be part and parcel of its charm.

As Graham went about his task, she watched him idly. He was an outdoorsman. She could see it in the way he deftly tugged at several stray boards by the back door, in the way he easily sidestepped the exposed tree root over which the realtor had taken an embarrassing fall, in the way he vaulted over a portion of the fence that kept him from the carriage house.

With a deep breath of the clean, cool air, she conjured images of Jason trying to survive in rusticity. Never! she mused, then glanced again at her watch. It was nearly twelve-thirty. Another hour left. Would Graham be finished in time? She really didn't want to have to go into explanations about her job. Not today. Not to this man. Indeed, whoever took the job would quickly learn that for an hour every afternoon she was indisposed. But the fewer people who knew, the better. She had no idea how her work would be received.

Bent on coaxing him inside with the lure of a cup of coffee, Debra rose from the swing and caught up with Graham in front of the carriage house. But his deep involvement with the matter at hand diverted her. "I thought I'd make this into a garage," she said, "with plenty of storage space. What do you think?"

He waited until he'd finished writing. "I think that might be just right. If you wanted, you could enclose the breezeway so you could reach your car without having to go outside. I've seen it done, but—"

"That would interrupt the flow of air from front yard to back, not to mention ruining the full effect of the roses I was told would blossom pretty soon. No, thanks. I'll leave it as is."

"Good" was all he said. But his eyes held obvious approval as he looked her way. They were warm, amber, and perceptive. Debra had the sudden feeling that he could see beneath her layers much as he could those of her house. Turning awkwardly, she headed indoors, only then recalling her intent.

"Would you like some coffee?" she called back over her shoulder. When he didn't answer, she looked around. "Graham?" His head was bent, his frown deep. "Coffee, Graham?"

As if hearing her for the first time, he looked up, startled. "Uh, no. No, thanks." Then he thought again. "On second thought, maybe I will. If it's no trouble."

"No trouble," she murmured, continuing on her way.

It was fully ten minutes later that Graham followed, knocking tentatively, though the door was ajar, standing head down, deep in thought, until she appeared and gestured him in. His hesitation was so subtle that she couldn't have detected it any more than he could have prevented it. But he knew he'd take the step. One part of him had already fallen in love with her house.

He remained for a minute in the front hall, taking his first good look at the inside of the house before trailing Debra to the carton-strewn kitchen. "Whew," he exclaimed, "this isn't exactly what I'd call efficient." He shot successive glances, one more discouraged than the next, at the mélange of shelves and cabinets that seemed to have been inserted as needed. "I'd tear it all out. In fact," he said with a sweeping glance up and back that implied inclusion of the whole of the house, "I'd tear out *most* of the place. It may be large, but if the upstairs is at all like what I've glimpsed down here, it's chopped into so many small pieces that you feel closed in everywhere."

Extending a steaming mug in his direction, Debra leaned back against the old porcelain sink. "Some call it cozy." She smiled. "But I happen to agree with you. I've spent too many years living in apartments to want to be boxed in again. I'd like to break down most of these walls, perhaps leave half walls here and there"— she pointed—"like between the kitchen and dining room." Sipping her drink, she watched for Graham's reaction. "I'd also like to open up the second floor— you know, give the living room a cathedral ceiling by demolishing one of those four bedrooms, open up at least another one of them into a recreational loft overlooking everything. What do you say?"

"About the possibilities?" His eyes were alight. "They're endless."

"About *your* doing it."

He cleared his throat, and the light dimmed. "I don't know. I'll have to do more figuring." By the time he raised the mug to his lips, his gaze was dark. He kicked a booted foot out at one of the cartons. "You brought all this stuff with you?"

"Uh-huh. I figured I'd need something to get me going." She followed his gaze to the enameled pots and pans peering from one box. "The only problem is that I can't bear to unpack. It's like cleaning. Everything will have to be taken out, anyway, once the work begins. And while *that's* going on, the entire house will be filthy." She scowled. "Come. Let's go into the living room. My fire's apt to die on me if I don't give it some attention."

Leading the way, she gave momentary consideration to the tiny flicker of apprehension that surfaced at odd times. It wasn't really fear, or was it? Though this move had been her dream for so long, she hadn't quite imagined it under these circumstances. In her mind, it had always been something she and Jason would do together. Strangely, Graham's presence, imposing to say the least, made her all the more aware of the utter quiet she'd lived with the night before. Yes, she wanted the quiet; it was a welcome change from the steady diet of city sounds on which she'd always lived. But it was also representative of how alone—physically alone— she truly was. There was no one around for miles. And *that* was a totally new experience.

"I'm sorry I can't offer you much of a seat," she murmured with a gesture toward the bare floor. "Nothing's arrived yet." Putting down her coffee, she deftly gathered her papers into a pile and put them atop her typewriter case as unobtrusively as possible. To her relief, Graham was too busy shoring up the fire to have noticed the move. She took the opportunity to peek at her watch. Another fifteen minutes had passed. Time was getting shorter. Settling on the floor before the fire, she retrieved her coffee.

"Will you take the job?" she asked bluntly.

For all outward signs, Graham hadn't heard her. He stood examining the marble mantel. "This is beautiful. It should be cleaned and polished."

"That's what I was planning to do. I thought I'd paint the bricks around it white. In fact, I'd like to do most of the house in white. It's so much more airy and open than the dark colors they seemed to have loved back then."

"Dark colors were more practical then." One corner of his mouth curved. "Those homemakers didn't have the white tornado on their side." Propping an elbow on the mantel, he slowly lifted the mug to his lips.

Debra watched him, feeling his strength even from where she sat. His fingers curved easily around the cup, their nails trim and well scrubbed. He was a carpenter, good with his hands. Quite irrelevantly, she wondered how good he really was, what other things those lean fingers could hold, what they'd feel like against her own. Clenching her hand into a fist, she looked away.

"Well? How about it?" she asked. "Will you do it?"

He took another long, leisurely sip, then lowered the mug and wiped his upper lip with his lower one. "I don't know. I still have to go through the inside of the house and then take my notes back to study. Then I have to draw up some plans."

"But you *are* considering it, aren't you?"

His jaw flexed in a move she interpreted as impatience. "I wouldn't be here if I weren't. But"—he paused, his voice dangerously quiet—"you shouldn't be so eager, you know. I could easily take advantage of your enthusiasm by accepting your job here and now, taking a huge retainer, then rushing the work off sloppily."

"You wouldn't do that," she argued with a mystical sense of conviction.

"How do you know?" he retorted. "You don't know me."

"Then tell me about you. How long have you been doing this type of work?"

Chagrined that he'd led himself into such a fast trap, Graham frowned and swirled the coffee remaining in his cup. If he cared to be exact, he mused, he'd be stuck with long explanations. It was far better that she assume him to be only a carpenter. "Nearly twenty years," he answered, broadly interpreting "this type of work" to include the designing he'd done in school.

"Have you always lived here?"

"No."

When he stared at her stonily, she knew he'd say no more. She wondered in that instant, as she had the day before, if he hadn't a side entirely different from the one he showed the world. If that were true, she'd be wise to chalk her fascination up to morbid curiosity and let it go at that. Much as she might be intrigued by the physical nature of the man, she told herself in warning as much as anything, she wanted no part of such complexity. She'd left the city in search of simplicity. And simplicity was what she'd get, damn it!

"Well, then," she resumed with a sigh, abundantly aware that it had to be nearing one o'clock, "I guess you'll just have to do your looking and come back to me with a proposal and estimates. As for the quality of your work, I have no question. If you want the job, you've got it." She paused, smiling. "I may be a newcomer around here, but it's my guess that word of mouth *is* your best advertising. I doubt you'd do a sloppy job for me—for that reason and for the reason that you seem far too dedicated. The proof of the pudding is in the eating; those finished products I saw were scrumptious."

"'Scrumptious'?" he repeated, wincing. "I've never thought of my work as being scrumptious. Better keep that to yourself; it could do more harm than good."

She grinned. "To the old macho image?"

"You bet." The look he cast her at that moment did the old macho image proud. Its power was shattering, suffusing her body with an awareness that stunned her. Her breath caught in her throat; her pulse accelerated. A heat surged through her veins, finding outlet only in the flush on her cheeks. As she'd been before, though to a far greater degree now, she was struck by his raw virility. Yes, virility. Before, she'd called it carnality or earthiness. Now it was virility. He was all male. Without a doubt.

Suddenly frightened, she averted her eyes. But the current of sensual awareness was not as fast to dissipate as she'd hoped. It lingered through the silence, then sizzled all the hotter when Graham hunkered down and tipped up her chin. His finger was strong; she couldn't have fought it. Raising her eyes to his, their gazes locked.

"Do you now understand why I have reservations about accepting this job, Debra?" The pad of his thumb moved gently back and forth, then pressed when she didn't answer. "Do you?"

"I'm nothing to you."

"You're a beautiful woman."

She could barely breathe, he was that close. "Not beautiful. I have eyes."

"The eyes of a woman. Through a man's eyes, you're beautiful."

"Not necessarily," she whispered back, recalling how easily Jason had turned his back on her. He'd found his leading lady much more beautiful.

"Yes," came the insistent reply from lips that inched closer while the fire crackled. Debra slowly shook her head, part in denial of what he'd said, part in denial of what she knew to be happening. But he simply whispered it again, a soft "Yes" against her lips, before he kissed her.

Later, Debra was to wonder how it had happened. There was nothing remotely romantic about the scene —an unfurnished, time-worn living room in broad daylight with a fire for warmth and little else. But his lips touched hers with a sweet introduction that was the most romantic thing she'd ever known. She sensed it to be the handshake they'd been unable to exchange the day before . . . but a handshake in commencement of a relationship far different from the one she'd expected when she'd first sought him out.

When he raised his head to study her startled expression, he slid his hands to her shoulders and drew her closer. His eyes caressed her face, urging a silent "Kiss me" at every stop. By the time his gaze touched her mouth, she felt drugged. Lips parting helplessly, she watched him lower his head to kiss her again. Then, letting her lids lower and close, she thrust all thought aside to simply savor the delicious warmth of him as he tasted her lips a second time. His lips moved cautiously, exploring each curve and corner as if half-expecting to find a thorn. When they didn't, he grew bolder, lightly tracing the shape of her mouth with his tongue, leaving a moist path in its wake.

In a burst of indulgence quite without guilt, Debra let herself go. Having breached a barrier of formality, she gave rein to her impulse to find out about this man. Her kiss, returned with the same gentle curiosity, was as much one of discovery about herself as about him. But when, curiosity unsated, she slid the tip of her tongue to meet his, they both jumped.

Firmly pushing against her shoulders, Graham managed to simultaneously force her lower while he stood. "Beautiful . . . and dangerous," he muttered hoarsely. "A forbidding combination."

Debra struggled to catch her breath. "It doesn't . . . need to be," she gasped, knowing that, more than ever, she wanted him to rebuild her house. She didn't stop to think why, any more than she stopped to consider her words before she spoke. "There's always . . . self-restraint."

"Hah! What do you think that *was?*" Hands on his hips, he glared down at her. "Without it, we'd be well on our way toward making love right now. And that's my point. You may say you're not beautiful, but my body says otherwise. And it's not going to let me forget it!" Cursing softly, he turned, put both elbows on the mantel and buried his fingers in his hair.

Watching the painful rise and fall of his shoulders as he sought further control, Debra tried to agree with his judgment. Her own body still tingled; perhaps it *would* be better if she found another carpenter. But she couldn't. Graham was the one she wanted.

"I'm not a child," she reminded him, her voice finally even. "I can exert some control of my own."

"Like you did just now?" He didn't turn.

"I, uh, wasn't prepared just now." He was a stranger, for God's sake! A workman—a carpenter! She'd never done anything like this before. "It just . . . happened."

He slanted a glance toward where she knelt. "And you don't think other things will just . . . happen?"

"Not if we don't want them to." Mind over matter, so to speak.

"But we do!" he growled. "At least, *I* do. I'm a man, Debra. One look at you yesterday and the juices started flowing. Sure, right now, with my mind in control, I'm bothered by the thought of rolling on the floor with a prospective client. But, to be honest, I don't know how far I can trust that quirk of conscience. If I were to work here day after day—well, I wouldn't want to take responsibility for my actions."

"I'll take that responsibility." She rocked back on her feet and stood quickly, growing all the more firm against Graham's warning. "I want the best carpenter. You happen to be it." She tipped up her chin. "Will you or will you not take the job?"

For a minute, Graham simply stared at her, his eyes narrowed in skepticism. The same doubt was in his voice when he spoke. "Have you heard anything I've said, Debra?"

"I've heard."

"And . . . it doesn't bother you . . . the idea that I could be working around your house plotting where and when I can grab you?"

"I can handle that," she vowed. "What I can't handle is the thought of a second-rate somebody doing a second-rate job on my house. Now, if you think you can do better than that, you've got the job."

Graham lifted a hand to scratch the back of his head. "That sounds like a challenge," he said, his voice dead calm.

"I'd say it was a challenge," she acknowledged, growing bolder by the minute. " . . . Are you up for it?"

"Poor choice of words."

"Damn it," she cried in exasperation. *"Do you want the job?"*

"Yes!" he growled. "I want it."

Brow furrowed in frustration, she threw her hands into the air. "Thank God! Now we're getting somewhere!" She had no idea how her show of spirit enlivened her expression. Graham did. With only the slightest flicker in his eye to hint at mischief, he reached out and pulled her into his arms, against the full length of his body. "What are you doing?" she cried in alarm, unable to believe he'd go through with it.

"Kissing you," he whispered, and settled his mouth warmly, seductively over hers.

"Graham, stop!" she protested, twisting her lips away to let the breathy words escape. It was a matter of principle; she had to demonstrate self-control. Flattening her hands on his chest, she pushed, but he was immovable. "Graham . . ."

He dragged his lips across her cheek to nibble at her ear. "Uh-huh?"

"Let me go."

"Why?"

"Because . . . because I have something to do." More critically, she feared her self-control would prove flimsy. The feel of his body excited her more than she cared to admit.

He drew back his head in surprise. "Oh? I'm keeping you?"

She managed to wedge a greater distance between them by making a show of looking at her watch. It was one-twenty-five. "Yes."

"Well, then." He cleared his throat and set her back, holding her waist for several seconds before dropping his hands to his sides. "I won't hold you up."

Time was getting short. Debra wanted him gone. But her momentary wave of relief proved premature. She was dismayed to hear him add, "Do you mind if I just wander around a little more? I'll need to take some measurements and see the basement. In fact, I really haven't done much looking in here . . . at the right things, that is." The gleam in his eye told all. She struggled to stay calm.

"Uh, you want to do all that today?"

"Sure. And we should really talk more. I can come

up with my own plans, but it would help if you told me as many of your ideas as possible just to give me some insight as to what you do or don't want."

Unsure as to whether he was now the consummate professional or whether he was simply mocking her, she nodded. "You're right, of course. And the sooner you get the information you need, the sooner you can begin. When *do* you think you can start?"

He tapped the eraser end of the pencil against his forehead. "It'll take me another three, at most four, days to finish up at the bank."

"The bank?"

"I've been doing some remodeling there."

"All by yourself?"

"Actually, I'm kind of supervising the thing. Which is why I've been able to take off yesterday and today. I'm itching to get back to working with my hands, though," he drawled. For all the innocence of his expression, his tone dripped of roguery.

Debra steadfastly ignored his bait. "So I can imagine. Then you think you'll be able to start next week?"

"If I get the plans drawn up and if you agree to them and if I can get hold of the things I need. I'll start with demolition—tearing down walls, wading through layers of what's been put on before. And I'll have to spend some time lining up jobbers—you know, getting the plumber and electrician over here." He arched a brow in warning. "It might get pretty busy."

"So much the better," she returned, knowing that safety would come with numbers. "But, uh, I'll need somewhere to work. Is there a particular room you can leave until last?"

He'd heard her refer several times to her work. Now his curiosity got the better of him. "What kind of work do you do?"

It was one-thirty. Debra could feel it in her bones. She wished he'd get going so she could watch the show.

"I write," she said quickly, hoping he'd nod and move on. But he didn't.

"Ah." The exclamation was exaggerated and accompanied by a smug glint. He seemed to have all the time in the world. "One of those."

"What do you mean?"

"We get them up here every so often. Writers, would-be writers. All seeking inspiration from the fresh country air."

It certainly wasn't why *she'd* come, but she was just as happy to let him believe what he wished. In fact, she was beginning to feel more reckless by the minute. If she was going to have to turn on the television every day, he'd know it soon enough.

"We'll see if it works," she said, all the while knowing that Graham Reid and his damned virility would be far more inspiration for her work than the fresh country air. "Now, there's something I've really got to do. If you'll excuse me?"

It was as blunt an invitation for him to leave as she could have made. Graham eyed her, puzzled. "May I look downstairs?"

She didn't move. "Be my guest. It's not much more than a hole in the ground with a furnace and a lot of pipes. Maybe they'll make more sense to you than they did to me." She spoke more quickly than usual. "It's the small door beside the stove in the kitchen. Watch your head."

He sent her a wry smile. "Thanks."

The instant he disappeared, she hurriedly knelt to open the miniature television-radio console that had stood innocently by her suitcases looking for all practical purposes like simply another leather-bound case. Not so. This gem had been a gift to herself when she'd returned from Haiti with the divorce decree. Running on batteries, it was symbolic of the severance of her long-held New York ties. The only ties now would be through the postal service, an occasional phone call to her producer and this small screen on which the words she'd written would come to life.

The excitement had never waned, though she'd been writing scripts for nearly six years. There was something about seeing her characters, her dialogue, her own depiction of triumphs and traumas, broadcast from coast to coast to an audience of millions. "Love Games" was not the longest-running soap opera by any means. It had, however, done surprisingly well from the first, making it one of the most popular—and responsible for the demise of two others since.

Even after watching the show so very many times, she was still startled to see *her* name listed at the end with the credits. Hers . . . and Jason's . . . and the five other writers who rounded out the crew. When she'd started at age twenty-four, she'd been the youngest, and despite what had happened since, she owed much of her good fortune to Jason. He'd encouraged her to help him out week after week until she was finally accepted as a legitimate member of the team. To this day, Debra was convinced that Jason had been as pleased as she with that development. Their own problems had come later.

But there were other problems to be considered now. Fine tuning the small television picture, she adjusted the volume through the overture, then watched as the story picked up where it had left off the day before, with an irate Jonathan Gable discovering that his wife, Selena, had disappeared again. Yes, that was good, just the way Debra had envisioned it, with Jonathan careful to let the world think his annoyance was directed solely at the burly watchdog he'd hired to avoid this type of thing.

In essence, he was furious at his wife. This was the petty form of punishment she inflicted, a pouting plea for attention, each time she suspected him of having a new affair. Perhaps in the past her suspicions had been correct; this time they were not. The woman he'd been seeing on the sly was most probably his half-sister, the child his father had denied for forty-eight long years. But he didn't yet know for sure. And he certainly couldn't tell Selena. The woman was her own father's newly acquired companion.

Disgusted, Jonathan cursed Selena and her childishness. Her periodic retreats caused him nothing but embarrassment and the inconvenience of having first to find her, then fetch her from her self-imposed exile. He would have divorced her years ago had it not been for her father's fearsome political power. Granted, he was aging, the old man was, yet to Jonathan's everlasting chagrin, he remained very much in the political picture.

Selena Gable knew she had her husband in a bind. His electronics interests had flourished in large part through government-sponsored contracts that her father had been instrumental in securing. Without the contracts, which were regularly up for renewal, the business would suffer, if not fail. Selena thrived on that knowledge. Her father's power was her only hold over Jonathan, whose physical interest in her had waned years ago. She didn't want a divorce. Gable Electronics was a gold mine and was to go to her three children *equally;* she wanted that more than anything. Jonathan already suspected that the youngest, Ben, was not his son. But as long as the marriage stayed intact, he would say and do nothing. As long as either of his two legitimate children had a stake in Gable Electronics, he *couldn't* say anything. He and Selena were on a merry-go-round, one horse higher, one lower, ever alternating in an agonizingly repetitive cycle from which neither could escape for fear of falling under oncoming hoofs.

Then there was Adam Gable, their oldest son and a lawyer by profession. It was Adam whom his father now called to the helm while he took off in search of his wife. Adam was quite used to taking over for his father, and possessing an inherited thirst for power, did so eagerly. Now, with his father's absence, he had his chance. Rushing back to his own office, he called the director of the Fielder Institute, a good friend, with instructions to have the contracts drawn up and sent over. His father had resisted involvement in brain implants for far too long. It was time Gable Electronics took its turn, and the timing couldn't have been better. If he signed the agreements within the week, a major competitor would be cut off. Adam cared little that the competitor's president was an old friend of his father's and deserved fair warning. It was his firm belief that the success of the initial work—and the subsequent business it would generate—would compensate, in Jonathan Gable's mind, for the audacity of his move.

Debra knew better, but only because the script she wrote today was that much further ahead in the story line. As Adam Gable's face yielded to a boisterous ad for laundry detergent, she lowered her knuckles from her mouth, took a deep breath and straightened. To anyone watching, she must have looked like an addict, neither moving nor speaking while the drama had unfolded. But no one *was* watching, or so she had thought.

Feeling suddenly hot under the collar, she slowly looked toward the hall. There, propped against the doorjamb, stood Graham, wearing a look of irritation not much different from the one Jonathan Gable had worn at the start of the show.

Chapter Three

"I have to admit that I've never been shafted in favor of a soap opera before," he gritted. "This was what you 'really had to do'?"

There seemed no choice but to confess, which Debra proceeded to do on a note of indignation. Graham was, after all, only her carpenter. Provided she was willing to pay his bill, she could keep him waiting for whatever reason she wanted.

"Yes. It's an important part of my day."

"You're kidding!"

"Not at all."

"You watch the soaps every afternoon?"

He might as well know it now. "Just this one . . . every afternoon."

"It's got something special going for it?" His lips curved into a mocking half-smile that hardened her all the more.

"You could say that." He should only know.

Shaking his head, he released a sigh of amazement. "God, I'd never have pegged you for a diehard soap opera fan! You're full of surprises, aren't you!"

"Not really," Debra said, then shrugged and turned back to the television with feigned nonchalance. "You just don't know me very well." The second segment was beginning. Let Graham think what he would. She was determined to watch.

Her back to him in determination, she missed the enigmatic expression that crossed his face. He certainly *didn't* know her very well, but what little he did know bewildered him. Was she the cool sophisticate from New York who was trying her hand at country life or the free-spirited writer in jeans, a sweatshirt and pony tail? And what about this waif whose afternoon revolved around the ups and downs of a soap opera? A *soap opera!*

Debra didn't seem to fit into any given mold, and in that sense she disturbed him. That sense . . . and others. Even when she ignored him completely, as she did now, he was aware of the gentle curve of her shoulder, the straightness of her back, the slimness of her legs as they curled beneath her and held her meager weight.

Turning on his heel, he made his way upstairs, absently analyzing the condition of the old oak treads, quickly despairing of the rickety banister. He was crazy, he told himself. He should never have taken the job. It wasn't only that he'd be physically tormented by her presence. But she bothered him in odd ways, evoking, among other things, an uncanny protectiveness in him. So *what* if she was cold? She should have known enough to get her own coat! So *what* if the place was primitive? She knew what she was getting when she'd bought the house. Why should he be the one to worry?

What *did* worry him was that he reacted to her more strongly than he had to any woman since he'd left New York. Yes, he'd do her job for as long as it took, spending day after day around her, perhaps getting to know her, in all likelihood finding his way to her bed. But what then? Would he be able to pack up his tools and leave when the job was done? Furthermore, would she *let* him? He'd felt her response when he'd kissed her; he'd sworn she was as hungry as he. And women were possessive when it came to men. He knew that all too well. Not, given the circumstances, that he regretted having married Joanie; it had been his responsibility, something he would have done even had her father *not* insisted on the wedding. But he still suspected that Joanie's "accident" had been far from an accident. She had wanted to trap him; she'd done so in a way she had known he couldn't fight.

Now came Debra Barry, booking six months of his life. He'd warned her, but she'd been firm in taking full responsibility for whatever happened—or didn't—between them. She was either a saint or a sinner, or she really *did* admire his work. She knew what she wanted; her ideas were good. They needed modification, of course. And then, he had a slew of ideas himself. Working together, they might easily produce her dream house. Somehow that mattered very much to him.

Standing in the smallest of the four bedrooms, looking out at the back yard and the meadow beyond, he thought of his own house, hidden behind a curtain of trees on the far side of the mountain. He'd built it from scratch, slowly, living out of his pickup when he'd first moved here seven years ago. Funny that he should worry about Debra roughing it in her own house! Even funnier that his reasoning had been the same; he'd been new to the area, hadn't known anyone and had rebelled against staying in a motel. Once a week for a shower was fine. The lake at the foot of the mountain did wonders in between. If he'd looked and smelled like a workman, so be it. His three-piece-suit days, days of looking down on the city from the forty-fourth floor, were over. He was on the ground floor to stay. All things considered, he preferred the view.

Opening his notebook, he moved from room to room, examining the walls, windows, floors and ceilings, making voluminous notes on his findings. Time and again he extended his tape to record the dimensions of an area. Time and again he found his excitement on the rise with the advent of one new idea or another.

Lost in his art, he didn't notice the hour. When he finally returned to the living room, he found Debra frowning before a dark screen. "Something happen to your TV?"

She looked around in surprise, having been thoroughly engrossed in her own art. "Uh, no. The show's over."

"And that's cause for depression?" He still couldn't believe she'd been watching what she had.

She turned on him with a vengeance that perplexed him all the more. "Only when really dumb things happen! I mean, I know that these cases of amnesia tend to get boring, but to spice the plot up with incest—that's carrying innovation a little too far!"

He shrugged. "Doesn't sound so far-fetched to me. I thought that was standard fare for soap operas. The raunchier the better."

Leaning forward, she folded the television into its case and snapped it shut. "That's the image, isn't it?" Scowling, she scrambled to her feet. "Well, there are some of us who disapprove of it. We see a difference between realism and absurdity, and we much prefer the first! Stooping to the lowest accomplishes nothing beyond insulting the viewer's intelligence!"

As Graham struggled to comprehend her outburst, so he struggled to contain his amusement at its force. "You could always write a letter," he offered half in jest, to which she responded with a smooth, smug drawl.

"I can do better than that!" But she'd barely taken two steps when she stopped, a stricken look on her face.

"What's wrong?"

"The telephone," she moaned. "It won't be in till tomorrow."

"You were going to *call* them?" he asked in disbelief, and let out a hearty laugh. "A crusader in the backwoods!" Then he feigned instant sobriety, lowering his voice conspiratorially. "Do you do this type of thing often?"

It was his laugh, so rich and full, that had done it. Suddenly, it seemed less critical that she objected to Martin Alonzion's manipulation of the story line. That was a matter for Martin and Harris, a matter for New York. She was no longer there.

Her face softened with a poignant indulgence. "It's strange. I never used to say a word. I guess I'm getting feisty in my old age."

"Old age, my foot. Today you look about eighteen." As soon as he heard the words, he flinched. His own daughter turned eighteen in another few months. Suddenly, he wondered how old Debra Barry *was*.

When she smiled, her eyes sparkled. "Now that's the nicest thing you could've said to me, considering that I turned thirty last week."

An overwhelming sense of relief surged through him. At least it wouldn't be like seducing a friend of his daughter! "Did it bother you, turning thirty?"

"Not until last night, or rather this morning." Her gaze shot to her belongings in the corner. "That sleeping bag may have conquered the cold, but it sure was helpless against the hardwood floor." She flexed her shoulders experimentally. "It's better now, thank goodness."

Graham reached out. "Here, let me see."

But Debra was fast to step out of reach. "It's all right!" She feared what would happen if he touched her. Those long, lean fingers were far too skilled. "I'm fine."

"You keep saying that, yet first you're cold, now stiff—"

"I'm *not* cold. And as for the stiffness, I'll get used to it."

"You're not planning on sleeping on the floor until the work is done, are you?" he asked with such an appalled expression that Debra couldn't restrain herself.

"What's the matter, Graham? Don't tell me that would discourage *you?*" He was a hardy man of the flesh, the American cowboy come East. She could almost picture him camping out, with his trusty brown pickup ground-hitched nearby.

"Are . . . you . . . kidding?" His deep drawl gave credence to the image. "Let me tell you, babe, *nothing* discourages me when I want something."

Only then, with the knavish glint in his eye, did Debra latch onto his meaning. Ruing the blush that stole to her cheeks, she chided him. "That wasn't what I meant. And it's Debra, not 'babe.' Don't tell me New Hampshire women like these little nicknames because I won't believe you."

He shrugged. "Then I won't tell you. But . . . don't you think that you're going a little too far with this roughing-it business? I mean, adventure is fine now and again. Cold-turkey withdrawal is something else. If you think one night made you stiff, give it a couple more. And while we're on the subject"—he shot her a sideways glance—"if that is supposed to be a desk, you'll be crippled before the week is out."

"Graham," she mocked, not quite knowing what else to do, "I didn't know you cared."

"If you're paying the bills, honey, I can be very protective."

She sighed. "Ah, so that's the way it is. Well, then, you can rest assured that my bed will be delivered soon. And as for a desk, I'll see about buying one if you can tell me where to set it up. You never did answer my question."

"Which one?"

"About a little corner to live in while the work is going on?"

"You're really determined to live here through it all?"

"Yes."

Glancing around the room, he grew thoughtful. Then, turning, he backtracked to the stairs, where he paused for a moment's consideration before bypassing them to continue on into the kitchen. Debra followed close on his heels, nearly barreling into him when he abruptly stopped at the entrance to the rear addition.

"Here?"

After an instant's deliberation, he shook his head. "No. There's too much I want to do here." And he stepped past her to go out the back door. "I'll be right back."

But she was right behind, keeping pace as he crossed through the breezeway. "The carriage house?"

"Could be fine." The door resisted him momentarily before opening with a whine.

It was dark. The only light came from the door they'd left ajar. The windows had long since been boarded up. "It's not much more than a barn!" she protested meekly.

But Graham was unfazed. "Come on. Where's your sense of adventure?" As his eyes adjusted to the dark, he crossed the floor to test the huge double doors. "They're solid. And it's relatively warm in here."

He was right. She'd noticed the warmth the instant they'd entered. The heavy wood walls kept out drafts, while keeping in heat generated by the sun on the roof. Or was the warmth she felt an awareness of Graham?

"What . . . what about electricity?" she asked. "I mean, there's no way I'd be able to work."

He came to stand beside her, his hands cocked on his hips. In the shaft of light that spilled in from the door, she caught his calculating look. "A line can easily be brought in." His eyes skimmed the back wall, then rose to the loft. "As a matter of fact"—he grinned smartly—"it would work out well. If we were going to spruce this place up for a proper garage and storage area, we'd have to put in new windowpanes, anyway. That gable door in the loft could be replaced with a large thermal dome, and with the other windows down here, you'd have a fair amount of natural light."

"I don't know," she murmured, needing that added bit of encouragement. Graham offered it readily.

"It'd be great!" he maintained, warming to his theme. "In a week I could have you set up here. You'd still have to go back to the house for running water—and to use the kitchen. But you'd be comfortable," he predicted, then dropped his voice, "and well out from under my feet."

"So there's reason for your madness, after all," she speculated, arching a brow in soft accusation. "You just don't want me in the way."

Graham tipped his head back and eyed the loft. "Actually, I was thinking of privacy."

"Hah! You forget that I'm used to people all over the place. Don't worry on *my* score."

He looked down into her eyes. "I was thinking more of *our* score." She caught her breath, but he went on. "There will be times when I'll have other people working in the house." His voice lowered. "And I really hate an audience."

Debra wished that the carriage house was lighter, colder, unsettling in some way. But it was quiet and cozy, dark and enveloping. "An audience would get very bored," she began, moving a step back. Graham reached out and caught her wrist.

"Would it?" He stepped forward, barely leaving

breathing room between them. When a gentle breeze toyed with the door, its shaft of light narrowed.

Self-control. Self-discipline. Debra silently stressed the words, as though they had the power to lessen the attraction she felt. But Graham stood tall and straight, his warmth alluring, his thumb drawing erotic designs on the soft inside of her wrist, in turn, sending waves of arousal through her veins.

"Graham . . . don't," she whispered.

"I warned you." His voice was warm velvet, deep as the darkness.

"You're doing this purposely, aren't you?"

"Yes." He inched imperceptibly closer.

She couldn't move. It was as if the dark braced her from behind, propping her as a pillow might, holding her in place. "Don't," she repeated in a wispy breath. "I . . ."

"You . . . what?" Very slowly, their bodies made contact. He drew her hand to the back of his waist and held it there. "Got something else you've 'really got to do'?"

She couldn't think of a blessed thing save the feel of her arm along the leanness of his waist. "I . . . should be . . . getting back to the house."

"No one will steal it." He dipped his head and growled against her cheek. "There's no one around . . . no one . . ."

His words and their quiet force were exciting beyond belief, dimming any hopes Debra might have had of pushing him away. She was alone, in a warm, dark carriage house, with an exceedingly virile man. As he towered over her, she felt his raw strength against her body, its latent power a vivid reminder of how he differed from the men she'd known before. He was a loner, a carpenter, and he turned her on with frightening power.

The thunderous beat of her heart seemed to be the

only sound. That, . . . and Graham's voice, deeper and more throaty now. "No one around to see what we do . . . or care." He brought his free hand to her neck. His thumb tipped her face up. "Kiss me," he ordered curtly.

She wanted to resist. She'd promised him. But . . . she couldn't. Beseechingly, she looked up at him, but he'd long since yielded the onus of restraint. It was a test, she knew, and she was about to fail with flying colors. Yet did it really matter? They were in the dark, and he was right; there was no one around. Who could care if she kissed her carpenter in the carriage house? After all she'd been through, who could begrudge her a brief flirtation with irresponsibility?

The tiniest whimper escaped her lips as they parted and rose to meet his. Her reward was the hungry reception she'd expected of him—the firm male lips that slanted greedily, the arms that lustily closed about her body, the wild heat that surged between them, welding them to one another.

"That's it, love," she heard him moan against her lips when he paused to shift her in his arms. "Come here," he rasped, then took her mouth again in a kiss whose vibrancy echoed through her body.

Finding her hand released, Debra slid it slowly up the taut line of his back. The sensation of sheathed steel was a heady lure to her other hand, which joined its mate in exploration. Graham was firm everywhere—firm and male. It was a potent combination.

And the darkness—the darkness seemed to heighten every sensation. Her blood throbbed in a hot surge through her veins; her body ached in fiery yearning. For as many times as she'd experienced passion with Jason, she'd known nothing that in any way approached the eroticism of this moment. She half-wondered if it were real, it was so very different. But then everything was different. She was a new woman and suddenly aware of the freedom her divorce had granted her. It was a perversely sobering thought. She was *single*. But *swinging*?

"Graham," she gasped, tearing her mouth from his. But he clasped her head and held her close, touching the tip of his tongue to her soft lower lip as she struggled to produce coherent sound. "Graham!" It was a wrenching plea, barely whispered with the meager shreds of strength he'd left her.

"Shhh . . ."

"No. You've got to stop."

"What about you?"

Her hands still clutched the bunched muscle of his shoulder. She forced herself to loosen their grip. "Me, too."

"Why?" He slipped his hands down to press her even closer. "We'd be good together. Don't you see?" His fingers traced the outer line of her thigh. She would have collapsed had not his other hand held her firm. "Come lie with me in the loft, Debra. Let's try it out."

"I can't," she wailed, wanting him desperately, knowing her need matched his. But it was physical . . . as was he. And she was an emotional creature. "Please, Graham . . ."

His answer was to lower his lips and seize hers angrily. She pushed against him then, but he pursued her relentlessly, forcing her mouth open, thrusting his tongue into its moist depths. And she let him. Much as she objected in principle to his force, she found it strangely exciting. When he set her abruptly back, her whole body trembled.

Sucking in a ragged breath, he glowered. "Maybe you should rethink hiring me. I want you, Debra."

"I know" was all she could say. She wanted him as well, but the words wouldn't come for fear of the consequences. Silently, she stood before him, her body aquiver. Yet when he reached out to touch her face, she didn't flinch. His fingers were gentle now, tracing the line of her jaw from ear to ear. His eyes followed the journey with their amber heat, flickering to meet hers for an instant before lowering to watch his hand cup her shoulder, then move on.

She felt herself sway; her blood rushed faster. When his palm slid down over her breast, she thought she'd die. That a touch, such a simple touch, should wreak such havoc in her body was frightening. Her chest rose and fell in agitation. Lips dry, she moistened them. But she couldn't move. Her feet were rooted to the floor, and her eyes—her eyes were sudden prisoners of marauding amber ones.

Slowly, his hand inched back and forth over the soft fabric of her sweatshirt. Her response was instant; he had to have felt it. Then he drew his thumb from the upper swell of her breast, with precision, down over its taut peak to its sensitive underside, and she bit her lip to keep from crying out.

Then his hand fell to his side, abruptly disengaged. The danger passed.

The same breeze that had cast them in darkness now blew open the door once more. In the harshness of the sudden light, Graham's expression seemed forbidding. His brows were drawn together, his jaw taut. The fire in his eyes flared with anger. "So much for responsibility," he scoffed; then he turned his back and stormed away. It was an about-face in more respects than one. When, from across the room, he eyed her again, he was remarkably cool, astoundingly dispassionate. "Well, Debra? What do you think?"

It took her a minute to find her voice. Even then it was faint. "About what?"

"Us." He stalked slowly forward, eyes on his prey. "You and me. Think we'll make it?" She couldn't help but recall the lion, waiting, ready to pounce at the slightest provocation despite his show of indifference.

"I think"—she took a cautious breath—"that the house will be great when it's done."

His voice was even. "What about the loft? Any hope for it?"

"And maybe you're right," she went on, daring to ignore his suggestive gaze to cast a nonchalant look of her own around. "This place will be fine for me while the other's being done." She paused. "Will you . . . do it?"

He gave an apathetic shrug. "I'm for hire."

Debra turned. "Then you're on." Squirreling her way through the door, she half-ran through the breeze-way, letting the battered screen of the kitchen's outer door slam behind her. When she reached the living room, she glanced frantically around for something to do. On impulse, she reached for a large log and dragged it toward the fire.

"Let me do that," Graham growled, coming up from behind to shoulder her aside. Within minutes, he had deftly rebuilt the fire to a healthy flame. "I'd stick to smaller logs if I were you. One like that is apt to drag you in with it."

"You'd like to think that, wouldn't you?" she asked, reacting to his condescension with a rebound of spirit. Since she evidently couldn't find it in herself to knee him, she'd simply have to learn to spit. Something, *anything* to redeem her pride. "You'd like to think that I can't manage without a man, wouldn't you? Well, you're wrong! You and—and *all* the men of the world who think of a woman as nothing more than a play-thing!"

His scowl grew more perplexed. "What?"

"Come on, Graham. 'Lie with me in the loft'? What kind of seductive line is that?" She happened to have found it devastatingly effective, but he shouldn't know that. "I've written any number of better ones, that's for sure!" With the spilling out of her words, she grew

appalled. In an attempt to cover her tracks, she raced
on. "And let me tell you something else. I could
probably match you night for night on the hardwood
floor, shiver for shiver in the chill, log for log on that
crumbling grate. What you may have brawnwise, I've
got right here." Making a fist, she hit her chest. "It's
called determination. Now"—she tossed her head back
as though having settled something—"when can you
start?"

Graham glared at her from the hearth in dark
reminder of the man who just yesterday had calmly
declined the job. For a minute, she thought he might
yet do so. He seemed furious as he gathered his pad,
pencil and measure from the mantel.

"I'll call you." He started for the door.

"But I haven't got a phone."

"You will tomorrow." He straddled the threshold.

"But you won't know the number!"

His answer was a terse "Information will." Pulling
the front door shut, he was gone.

When the phone rang late the following afternoon,
Debra felt the same visceral twitter that had taunted
her all night.

"Hello?"

But it wasn't Graham. Not by a long shot. "Debra!
It's about time! Do you know how worried I've been?"

She gritted her teeth. "No, mother, I don't. I told
you not to worry. I'm not *totally* helpless." The argument resumed at precisely the spot where it had left off
five days before when Debra had stopped in to say
good-by.

"I know you're not, but I'm your mother. I worry.
God knows what can happen to you off there in the
woods by yourself."

"I'm not in the woods."

"You know what I mean, Debra. Are you all right?"

"Of course I'm all right." Back against the wall, she slid down to the floor. "In fact, things are really great."

"Thank goodness! When I didn't hear from you, I—"

"Mother, I told you not to expect to hear from me for several *weeks!* I had no idea when I'd find a place."

"Tell me about it, darling. Is it . . . charming?"

"As in country?" Debra grinned. "I suppose you could call it that." She looked around; nothing had changed since yesterday other than that she'd written another day's script and mailed it off. Her grin turned wry. Funny thing about pent-up energy, she mused; when properly channeled, it could be quite productive. It had been a long night. "Actually, it was the potential of the house that appealed to me. It's very old and needs loads of work. I've already hired someone."

"You work fast."

So did he. "Uh . . . well, there wasn't much point in waiting. The sooner he starts, the sooner he'll be done."

"I don't know, Debra. Maybe you should have had Jason find someone he knows."

Debra stared straight ahead, focusing on a jagged crack that split the opposite wall. "Jason and I are divorced. I don't want or need his help. I'm managing very well on my own."

"But is he good, this fellow you've hired? Have you looked at his work and checked him out?"

"Yes, mother."

"And you're sure it's safe to have him in your house? I mean, you have to remember that you're up there alone. These craggy old craftsmen can be goats sometimes." Debra choked on a splintered breath and coughed. "Are you all right, dear? You're not getting sick, are you?"

"No, mother. I'm fine."

"It's been unseasonably cool here. I can imagine what it's like where you are. Are you warm enough?"

"I'm sitting right by the fire. It's delightful."

"Have your things arrived yet?"

"I just called the storage depot in Manchester. They'll be delivering everything on Monday."

"But what are you doing in the meanwhile?"

"I'm very comfortable, mother."

"Debra, you don't even have a bed!"

"Why is everyone so worried about where I sleep?"

"So Harris was after you, too?" Lucy Shipman asked, then rushed on, leaving Debra no time to alter the misconception. It was just as well; Graham's particular concern would have shaken her mother all the more. "You know, it was a good thing you finally gave him a call. He's been bugging Jason, wanting to know when you'd check in. He's counting on your continuing to write for the show."

"Yes, he told me. But I have every intention of doing so. It was never in doubt."

"Maybe not in *your* mind, but, well, you picked up and left so suddenly . . ."

It was one subject Debra didn't care to discuss. The knowledge of Jason's infidelity was too humiliating. "Sudden or not, my leaving hasn't inconvenienced Harris in the least. He'll get his script on time, just as he always has. Don't forget, I have a contract to fulfill."

"I'm sure Harris would give you more time if you need it, darling. You know how fond he is of you."

Not fond enough to warn her of impending mischief . . . or to do anything about it once it had begun. "Time isn't an issue here, mother," Debra countered rebelliously. "For once in my life, I've got as much as I need. And, frankly, I love it. But I *do* intend to get my work done. Don't forget, a contract works two ways. Harris gets his script; I get my money. Very honestly, I like the thought of being self-sufficient."

"If it's money you need, Jason would be more than willing—"

"I don't want Jason's money!"

"Then you know I'll help you out."

"Mother"—Debra sighed in exasperation—"I don't want your money, either. I was lucky. Despite a recent behavioral flaw that I'd rather not discuss, Jason was very good to me through more than five years of marriage. He insisted that I keep everything I earned in my name, either in the bank or in some sort of investment. I'm a wealthy woman in my own right." Not quite, but given the circumstances, a harmless stretching of the truth. "You'll just have to accept that." Somehow, Debra wasn't optimistic. Her mother had spent too many years controlling people to easily relinquish the reins on her daughter.

"I do, darling. But I worry. It's a mother's prerogative. After all, I'm not a youngster and—"

"You're fifty-four and in your prime," Debra interrupted with an indulgent smile. "And you look ten years younger. Pretty soon, they'll be confusing us for sisters."

"Not if you don't watch yourself up there, Debra. The air is dry. You have your moisturizer, don't you?"

At her mother's insistence, she'd had that since she was sixteen. "Yes, mother," she drawled, having long since learned not to argue. What she did when she hung up the phone was her own affair.

"Good!" the older woman exclaimed, apparently pleased that this most critical issue had been resolved. "Oh, and you will give Stuart a call, won't you?"

"Stuart? I was in touch with Stuart before I left. Is there a problem?"

"No. It's just that, well"—she took a breath and hurried on—"Stuart feels so badly about what happened."

Though he was her older brother, Debra had little

sympathy for him. "Stuart feels badly about the divorce? The fact that Jason played around didn't seem to bother him half as much!"

"Now, that's not true. He was *very* disappointed when he learned what Jason was doing. But he and Jason have been friends for years. He can't forget that, any more than he can forget how happy he was when the two of you married."

"So was I," Debra returned more sadly, "but things change. And it's foolish to try to recapture something that's . . . gone."

Lucy Shipman faltered for just a moment. "You don't love Jason anymore?"

"I'd rather not discuss this, mother."

"But if you love him—"

"We're divorced. It's over. *Over!*" Realizing how high her voice had risen, Debra tempered it quickly. "But enough about me. How are *you* doing?"

"I'll survive. Gardner's beginning to pressure me to set a date, but I'd rather not rush into anything." When Debra burst into a good-natured chuckle, her mother couldn't begrudge it. Her own smile came clearly over the line. "I know what you're thinking, daughter, and I suppose you're not all that wrong. I probably have rushed into things before. But I've reformed. Gardner may be my fourth, but believe me, if I decide to take him up on his proposal, he'll be my last. This constant name changing gets a little tedious."

"Ah, the life of a woman in demand!" Debra teased, but her mother's rejoinder sobered her.

"Like mother, like daughter. I've also had calls from John and Benjie, either of whom would like to see you when you're down. When will that be, darling?"

"I . . . I don't have any plans right now." Other than to steer religiously clear of New York, she thought.

"But I thought you'd be flying in at least once or twice a month to work with Harris."

"It's unnecessary. He'll mail me a weekly outline; I'll mail him back the finished script. Anything else can be settled by phone." It had taken some convincing, but with Debra's mind set, Harris had had little choice.

"What about Sandra's party? She's counting on you—"

"I called her last week and made my excuses. She understood perfectly." Hadn't Sandra been through a similar trauma herself several years ago?

"But surely you'll need to come back for more things . . ."

Lucy Shipman couldn't see her daughter's smug smile. "Not really. I've taken everything I want."

"But Jason says there's still a lot—"

"And I told Jason to get rid of it all. I'm gone, mother. Out!" The silence on the line spoke of her mother's dismay. Taking pity, Debra ventured on more gently. "And besides, I really can't get away now. Work on the house will be starting within the week. I'll have to be here to supervise."

"Won't all that sawing and hammering ruin your concentration? How can you work through that?"

Debra's enthusiasm surfaced on cue. "The setup here is perfect, mother. You see, there's the main house—where I am now—which is where most of the work is being done. Then there's an old carriage house that the carpenter is going to fix up for me to live and work in until the other is done. So I'll be away from the worst of it. There'll be nothing to bother me." Other than one Graham Reid. But she'd handle him. If there'd been one thing she'd decided after yesterday's fiasco in the dark, it had been to stay in the light with her eyes open . . . wide.

"Well, darling." Her mother sighed in reluctant

acknowledgment that her daughter seemed to have things under control. "I guess you know what you're doing. I'll miss you, though. You'll call, won't you?"

Though Debra knew that it would most probably be the other way around and frequently at that, she nodded. "Yes. I'll call. Once the house is finished, you'll have to come visit. You"—she grinned—"and ol' Gardner. I kind of like him."

"Thank heavens for that!" the other woman exclaimed facetiously, knowing that it really didn't matter. If she'd waited for Debra's approval, she'd have been single all these years. Debra was far too fussy for her own good. Indeed, it had been true cause for celebration when she'd finally fallen for Jason. And now they were divorced. Such a shame. "Now, Debra, you remember. If you get lonesome and want some company, I'll gladly pass the word on to Benjie. I like him better than John. A little classier. He'd be up there in a flash."

"Flashes are exactly what I don't need, mother, but thanks for the thought. Give my best to everyone, okay?"

"Sure, darling. You take care, now. Bye-bye."

As Debra hung up the phone, she felt a twinge of guilt. For all of her mother's idiosyncrasies, Lucy Shipman did worry. And it was no wonder the older woman had trouble accepting her daughter's declaration of independence; hadn't Debra played the game, more or less, for thirty years? But separation was better late than never, Debra mused, pushing away from the wall and standing with a boost.

And now what? She'd done her work for the day, the phone had been put in, and she'd dutifully called Harris to give him her number . . . then her mother had called. She'd have to remember to take Harris down a peg or two for that one.

What she needed was a hot cup of tea and the crossword puzzle. Heading to the kitchen for the former, she contemplated the latter. It was a tough one this week; all the more reason to have tucked it into her bag when she'd left New York. Perhaps sitting down fresh today, she'd be inspired.

The jangle of the phone jolted her, in part because of the newness of the sound reverberating around those walls, in part because of the sudden thought of Graham on the other end. Setting the teapot noisily atop a burner, she ran back to the living room. Having come straight off two calls from New York, she welcomed the thought of one verifying her new way of life.

"Hello?" she answered, carefully modulating her voice to conceal her eagerness.

"Debra! How are you?"

Her face fell momentarily. "Mike? I'm fine. . . . How did you get my number?"

"Mom just called. She thought you sounded a little down. Suggested I might cheer you up." He paused. "Might I?"

Michael Lang was her half-brother, her junior by three years. They'd always been close. "If I needed it, Mike, you'd be the one I'd call," Debra said with a smile, "but I'm great. You know mom—always looking for something that isn't there."

"I know, but I thought I'd check, anyway. Kind of liked the excuse to call. How *are* you? Mom said you'd already bought a house?"

Once again, Debra pressed her back to the wall and slid down to the floor. Once again, she told of her house, the work she hoped to do on it, her alternate living arrangements and her conviction that the move was the best thing she could have done.

"I really couldn't stick around, Mike. Not after—"

"I know. He's a rat."

"Stuart doesn't think so."

"That's because Stu's not much better. Why Stephanie stays with him is beyond me!"

"Well, I guess we can give him the benefit of the doubt. He *is* our brother."

"He's *your* brother. I only take *half*-credit."

"By the way, how's your dad?" Debra had always thought of the senior Michael as being far too weak for her mother. Perhaps he'd realized it himself. The woman he'd married after Lucy had divorced him had been a much more docile sort. They seemed far better suited to one another. And the marriage had lasted for nearly twenty years. That had to say something.

"Dad's fine. He and Marie are chasing the last of the snow in Aspen. They've become nuts about skiing."

"Must have caught some of it from you. By the way, if you ever want to camp out here en route to Tuckerman's Ravine, you know there's room."

"Mom was right. You're lonesome."

"I'm not lonesome. I'm simply enjoying the luxury of opening my house to guests of my *own* choice for a change. You should feel honored."

"I do, I do! But I think I'll have to wait till next winter for the skiing. I can't possibly get away until mid-May, and by then . . ."

"Well, the invitation's open all the same."

"You won't be back?" That same question, no less evocative the second time.

"Not in the immediate future. I'd rather the break be clean."

There was a brief pause, then Michael's soft voice. "For what it's worth, Deb, I think you're right. You deserve something better. I only hope you'll find it there."

She smiled her affection into her words. "Thanks, Mike. I know I will. Keep in touch."

Replacing the receiver, she put her head back against

the wall and inhaled deeply. There *would* be people she'd miss. Mike was one, her father another. On impulse, she raised the receiver, then put it down again. He'd still be in London. There was no sense even trying.

With the shrill cry of the teapot, she returned to the kitchen, only to have the phone ring before she'd even dug out a tea bag. Turning off the gas, she tripped back to the living room. It had to be Graham this time.

But it wasn't. "Debra?" The deep voice on the other end sounded vaguely cautious.

"Yes, Jason." She should have known.

"How are you?"

"Fine." She stood stiffly in the middle of the living room, the phone dangling from her hand.

"Harris gave me the number."

"So I figured."

"He . . . didn't see any problem."

"That's not surprising." She shifted her weight from one foot to the other.

"So," he picked up, "how are things going there?"

"Great."

"Got a nice place?"

"Uh-huh." She swung the phone idly. When it hit her thigh, she winced.

"Harris said you delivered on target. You're able to work?"

"Better than ever. It's quiet here. Perfectly delight-ful." Until he'd called. She deeply resented the intrusion.

"I'm glad." There was a pause. "Well, I just wanted to make sure you were all right."

She'd heard about enough. "You must have quite some guilty conscience."

"We're colleagues. Haven't I got a right to show interest?"

"I'm sorry, Jason. You yielded that right when you

took to Jackie's bed. I get so bogged down in the image of the on-set Lothario that I can't quite see you as a colleague."

Jason wasn't about to be put down so conclusively. He spoke smoothly, gently. "I just wanted to see what you thought of the show this week. I do respect your opinion, Debra."

"Not on all scores, but, yes, you always did when it came to our work."

"Did you like my stuff?" He knew how to reach her.

"How could I help but like it? You're the best they've got. Martin, on the other hand, is out in left field."

"That little incest thing bothered you?"

"Bothered me? Slightly! I saw nothing in the outline about that!"

"There wasn't . . . until Harris got the results of that new market survey. Remember, he told us . . . uh, no, you were away."

In Haiti. Obtaining a fast divorce. The silence was all the reply Debra made. Jason cleared his throat.

"Anyway, the survey claimed that we'd have to do something shocking if we hoped to keep up our ratings edge. We're still ahead, but if we want to stay that way . . . well, I guess incest is one way. And it wasn't all that bad when you consider that neither of the characters knew what they were doing."

"It was poor."

"Yah. Well, I'll mention it to Harris. Maybe that one shot will have been enough."

"God, I hope so."

Again, he paused. "Is there . . . is there anything you need?"

"Peace and quiet. This phone hasn't stopped ringing."

He ignored her quip. "I mean . . . do you . . . *need* anything?"

76

She knew precisely what he meant and felt no regret at disappointing him. "Nope."

"You're sure."

Never more so. "Uh-huh."

The voice on the other end grew more awkward. "Well, take care."

"I will." She didn't bother to return his quiet good-by, simply waited until its echo died before hanging up. It was several minutes before she unwound enough to set the phone on the floor. Then, gingerly massaging the tension from fingers that had clutched the instrument with unconscious vehemence, she scowled her annoyance and fumed toward the kitchen. When the phone rang again, she nearly screamed. Fists clenched, she stopped in her tracks, turned and seethed her way back to snatch impatiently the receiver from its hook.

"Hello!" It wasn't a question, but a demand.

For an instant, there was silence. Then his voice flowed over the wire, a bracing mountain stream, clear, running free and cool as the snow it had been not long before.

Chapter Four

$\mathcal{D}$ebra? It's Graham." His voice deepened in what she might have termed concern had she not known it to be impatience. He'd probably been trying the line. "Is everything all right there?"

She slowly exhaled. "It is now. Thank heavens you've called! Now I can just let it ring."

"Something's wrong?"

"They keep calling. I can't believe it! You'd think I'd been gone for months or that I was a total incompetent." She hadn't intended to subject Graham to her frustration. He'd simply caught her at a bad time.

"Who's 'they'?"

"You name it—Harris, my mother, Mike, even Jason. Actually, I was the one who called Harris. The others got the number from him."

There was a strange silence. Then in a blander tone, he said, "You're a popular lady. My apologies for bothering you."

"Oh, you're not!" she exclaimed, combing her fingers through her hair from the underside out. *"You're* the only one who's got something I want. Have you . . . have you made any progress on my plans?"

"That's why I'm calling." His business voice took over, no nonsense, to the point. "I spent a while on it last night and made some preliminary sketches. I've been out all day, or I would have done more. But I think I can get started on the carriage house early next week. I'd like to get you out of the main house as soon as possible."

Fleetingly, she recalled his threat of seduction in the loft, but as quickly decided that his formal tone precluded that. He simply wanted her out from underfoot. "You'll be able to start here as soon as I'm out?"

She could almost picture him shaking his head, ruffling the thick swatch of hair that seemed most natural brushing his brow. "Actually, that will depend on when I can get supplies. If I order things within the next few days, there might be a chance of it. But I'll have to discuss these plans with you before I put in an order."

"Of course. Say when."

"How does tomorrow afternoon sound?"

"Sounds fine. Uh . . . after two-thirty?" She'd nearly forgotten; how could that have happened?

Graham paused, then understood. "After two-thirty," he clipped. "See you then."

"Uh-huh. Bye."

Of all the calls she'd received in the past hour, this had been the most important, the most concise, the only one she'd been sorry to end. Graham suddenly seemed her link to the future. He represented all that was fresh and free, the antithesis of what she'd left behind. Particularly in the wake of that call from Jason, he was a welcome reminder of the break. She'd been right to insist on hiring him; she knew it.

Graham, on the other hand, hung up the phone with far less conviction that the decision he'd made had been right. Harris, Mike, Jason—was the woman living out a soap opera of her own? What *had* she run from, anyway?

But then, he mused, rocking back in his chair and bracing one foot against his desk, he wasn't one to throw stones. He had his own ghosts—very much alive. Propping a fist against his mouth, he studied the photograph that had arrived the week before. Jessie's high school graduation picture, sent to him by his father. Joan would have forbidden Jessie to send one herself, even if the child *had* thought to do it. But she hadn't. And she wasn't a child. Jessica. He'd have to start thinking of her as Jessica. She was a woman, nearly grown, no longer the tousle-haired child he used to cart off to bed.

Indulging himself momentarily, he recalled those days. They'd been a family then, a threesome, with Jessie too young to be aware of the tension existing between her parents. Only when she'd grown older had the charade begun to take its toll on her. Even now, his heart ached when he remembered the way she'd stood between Joan and him, looking from one to the other in confusion. How irrelevant the issues had been in the overall scheme of things—bedtime, allowance, summer camp—but they had been symptomatic of far deeper differences between husband and wife. Basic differences. Irreconcilable differences.

That was what they'd told the judge. On the surface, the divorce had been amicable. It was only later, as Jessie grew to be more and more of a stranger to him, that he realized the form Joanie's revenge would take. How ironic it was, he mused, even cruel. He'd married Joanie for the sake of his unborn child; when the marriage failed, he was to lose the child, after all.

His fist hit the desk with a dull thud, and he swung to his feet. It was this room that did it, this room that, of all those in his house, most faithfully reflected that other life. Books and digests lined the walls; papers blanketed the desk. And the photos—his parents, Jessie, his brother, Bob, and his wife—inspired a wave of melancholy for which there was but one remedy.

His footsteps were muffled by the carpet until he

reached the hall, where the soles of his shoes slapped the varnished oak, resounding through the silent house in eloquent testimony to his mood. It was only when he entered his sky-lit studio and slammed its door behind him that the noise ceased once more.

His hours in retreat were well spent; the plans he brought to Debra's house the following afternoon were spectacular, much more refined than the original ones. He knew it in his bones as he unrolled the blueprints, heard it in his words as he explained to Debra what he'd done, saw it in her eyes when they widened in delight.

"And we *can* use solar panels in back?" she asked excitedly, sitting on her haunches beside him on the floor.

"Sure." He smiled, pleasured by her enthusiasm. "It would be perfect. We can open up the two rooms of the addition to make the solarium you wanted. By building out here"—he propped himself on a knee and leaned forward to point to various parts of the diagram—"and here, we've got a pentagonal room. The roof slopes to the south, the one exposure where the tree covering is thin enough to let the sun through."

She nodded and studied the plans again, impressed by their thoroughly professional caliber. With care, she turned one page back to view the next, then shook her head in amazement. "I'd never have believed you could move the stairs."

"Most anything is *possible*. The question is whether you *want* them moved. The house itself, taken without its additions, is perfectly symmetrical. What you suggested you wanted to do with the second floor—opening part of it—will disturb that symmetry. Why not play up the change and really add some interest?"

Debra grinned. "Okay! I like it!" As she looked up at him, their shared vision was a near-tangible bond. In that instant, her heart tripped madly. In that instant, Graham seemed as touched. Then, with a deep in-drawn breath, he straightened.

"Have I forgotten anything?"

"Forgotten?" she echoed, dazed.

His expression hardened. "On the plans. Did I include everything you wanted?"

"That . . . and more! They're great, Graham. Thanks."

Averting his eyes, he simply dipped his head in acknowledgment of the compliment. "You keep these. I've got another set at home. If you think of anything, make note of it." He started to stand. "Oh, and I thought I'd drop by on Saturday to leave some things in the carriage house. Is that okay?"

It took her a minute to shift gears. "Saturday? Uh, sure, that's fine." Then she remembered. "Oh, but I may not be here! I thought I'd drive down to Manchester to pick up some things." After pausing for a breath, she went quickly on. "The door will be open, though. You can come, anyway."

He frowned. "You *always* leave the door open?"

"Not to this place." Her eye swept the room. "But the door to the carriage house has no lock. There's really nothing of value in it."

"There will be soon," he grumbled, his voice a mate to his stern expression. Whipping a pen from his pocket, he made the proper notation in his notebook, leaving Debra to cope with his darkening mood.

"I suppose you're right," she quipped lightly. "Around here, an intruder would be far more interest-ed in your tools than in my typewriter."

Graham didn't bother to correct her on the cause of his concern, merely pocketed the pen and notebook and turned to leave. She tried to think of something, anything to hold him longer . . . but could come up with nothing but the cause of *her* own concern.

"Graham?" She followed it through. He paused, his hand on the doorjamb, his back to her. "You're not still . . . reluctant . . . to take this job, are you?"

He hung his head, then looked back at her. His voice bore a numbing chill. "Of course I am. But I'll do it. Your damned house has me hooked. And you're right. Neither Forbes nor Campbell could have come up with those plans." Of course not. Neither Forbes nor Campbell had trained in New York, and much as Debra might deny it, she had a New Yorker's taste. Chic and sophisticated. Her house . . . and her. *Dangerous, Graham. Very dangerous.*

Debra heard the rev of the motor, the crunch of the tires, the roar of the engine and its fading as distance muted its sound. She sat and listened until there was nothing but silence. Then, chiding herself on her susceptibility to sturdy backwoodsmen, she rolled up the plans and set them aside for later study, flipped a fresh sheet of paper into the typewriter and began to list the things she'd want to buy in Manchester.

Her first purchase was perhaps the most exciting of the day. Having never owned a car before, much less a robust four-wheel-drive vehicle, she was initially cautious. With each stop, though—and there were many— she gained courage. By the time she turned in on the gravel drive at six that evening, the small rental car was forgotten and she and her shiny new Blazer were friends.

Packed comfortably into its rear load space were an assortment of purchases, ranging from heavy wool knee socks and a granite state sweatshirt to typing paper, mailing envelopes and peanut butter and jelly. Then there was the long slab of butcher block she'd chosen as a desk and the sturdy enamel tubes she'd had cut to size for its legs, the straight-backed chair she'd spotted at a garage sale and the cushions she'd subsequently bought for it and the thick down quilt of pale blue and cream that had very conveniently been on sale.

Sale or no, the last had been a splurge, given the fact that her electric blanket would be arriving with her things on Monday. Indeed, she'd idled at length in the bedding department before finally yielding to impulse. An electric blanket was practical and effective. A quilt, on the other hand, was cozy and comforting.

Hence, it was the quilt that she spread atop her large brass bed when the moving truck finally pulled away from the house Monday afternoon. Then, setting the small television before her and propping voluminous pillows behind her, she sat back to watch "Love Games." It was only at the break, between the second and third segments, that she realized she wasn't alone.

Graham stood lounging against the living-room door, an open soda can in his hand. He'd obviously raided her refrigerator, and she hadn't heard a thing. "You really get wrapped up in that, don't you?" he asked when her gaze flew to his in sudden recognition of his presence. "I've been standing here for five minutes. You make quite a picture lying there on the bed watching television. You're really going to sleep in the living room?" He tipped the can to his lips, though his eyes never left hers.

Shifting to a more dignified position, Debra rushed to her own defense. "It seemed to make the most sense. For one thing, the fire's here. For another, those stairs are narrow and closed in; the men would have had a terrible time getting this bed up to the second floor." It was queen-sized. "And finally, I'll be moving into the carriage house pretty soon. The bed will have to go there then."

He pondered her answer in its entirety for a minute,

then, seeming satisfied, dipped his head in salute. "Good thinking. And"—he raised the can—" thanks for the Mountain Dew." Turning, he retraced his steps to the back door and resumed his work in the carriage house, leaving Debra to recover from his impromptu visit.

Hugging her knees to her chest, she recalled his arrival that morning. His truck had been generously filled with building materials that he'd deftly transferred to the carriage house. She'd watched from an unobtrusive upper window, mesmerized by his sheer physical strength as he pulled, lifted and carried. Then he'd gone about his business as though she didn't exist. Not that she minded, she'd told herself when she turned from the window at last; she'd hired him to work, not to play. But she'd kind of hoped he'd stop to ask her how she was doing, whether she'd gotten her shopping done, even where she'd bought the Blazer.

He hadn't. He'd simply poured himself into his work with the same unswerving concentration he now seemed to criticize in her. Of course, he didn't know she was working, that she actually wrote the script she watched played out on the screen. Somehow she liked the idea of this little secret. It gave her an edge. At times, he seemed able to see so much, almost as though he knew just where she'd been.

And where had *he* been? Here in New Hampshire, in the shadow of the mountains, building things with those strong hands of his. Peering down at her own, she frowned. Where her skin was pale and smooth, his was darkened by wisps of hair. Where her fingers were slender and tapered, his were lean and blunt-ended. Where her palms were soft and pampered, his were bronzed and callused. So different . . . so exciting. But very much off limits. She'd have to remember that. He was her carpenter, and she was a woman on the rebound from a sudden and hurtful divorce. It was bad enough that her marriage had fallen apart. But to fool around with the hired help as she'd been strongly tempted to do that day in the dark of the carriage house . . . why, she'd be no better than one of her characters.

Recalling "Love Games," she returned to the present with a jolt and glanced at the set in time to find the show over for the day. She'd missed it! That hadn't happened since . . . had she *ever* missed it since she'd been writing? Thanks to the Betamax and Jason's diligent collection of tapes, she'd even been able to rerun the shows she'd missed while in Haiti. It was her job, she reasoned. And now she'd blown it!

Annoyed with herself, she bounded from the bed to the floor, taking a position before the makeshift desk that still held her typewriter, forcing herself to write an extra scene by way of punishment. And here she'd been worried about *Graham's* doing his job . . .

She was still pounding the keys when, two hours later, the man in question appeared once more. This time, his materialization beneath the living room arch caught her eye instantly. Hands suspended over the keys, she paused to send him a glance that bore the last remnants of self-reproach, before she typed on.

"You're working hard," he remarked offhandedly.

"I try." Eyes on the half-filled piece of typing paper, she struggled to hold to her train of thought.

"Is it the air?"

"Excuse me?" She mistyped a word, erased it, retyped.

"The fresh air," he drawled. "Is it true what they say about inspiration?"

She glanced up, then back down. "Oh, that." Then she sighed. "I really don't know. Inspiration has never been a problem for me." Her fingers seemed tireless, but off target. Ignoring another typo, then a third, she stubbornly continued. Head bent, she may have missed Graham's quizzical expression. She couldn't miss his ensuing taunt, however, soft as it was.

"A rare writer," he quipped. "You should pen your secret. It would be a best-seller."

Letting out a deep breath, Debra despaired of typing. She had at least one line of garbled nonsense already. Hands in loose fists on either side of her machine, she looked up. "Did you want me?"

For a split second, she thought he'd drawl a typically masculine response. The potential was there in his lazy stance, in his smug smile. Then the smile faded, and he drew himself up. "Actually"—his voice was level—"I wanted your phone. A local call. I'll make it fast."

Cocking her head toward the phone, which lay on the floor not far from her, she propped her arms behind her and sat back to watch as Graham lithely approached, hunkered down to dial and began to talk. His voice was low, his words brief and clipped; he looked at Debra all the while. When he was finished, he stood. "Thanks" was all he said before leaving.

For a long time, Debra didn't move, but sat staring in dismay at the spot where he'd knelt, recalling every last detail of his image. He wore what had to be his usual work outfit of jeans, a wool shirt and work shoes. Though nowhere near as dirty as he'd been that first day when she'd caught him working under his truck, he nonetheless showed signs of exertion in the casual disarray of his hair, the dark smudge of dirt branding his forearm, the pleasantly faint but distinct smell of man. Beneath his wool shirt, he wore an off-white thermal jersey; even now she recalled the way tawny bits of hair randomly escaped its loose crew neck.

Stifling a tingle, she bolted forward. But his image remained. Large, lean, commanding. The lion. Cool and aloof. For the first time, she wondered about his life. She assumed that the call he'd made had been business; the laconic half of the conversation she'd overheard implied as much. But she couldn't help wondering about the *non*business side of him. There had to be one. A man as blatantly virile as this one was bound to have women.

Her breath caught in the moment's realization that for all she knew, he was married, perhaps even with a slew of children at home. Oh, yes, he'd gone on about his disdain for New York women. But none of that talk precluded a wife; nor did that searing kiss he'd given her, or for that matter his suggestive eye on the loft. Jason had had a wife, and it hadn't stopped *him!*

With a burst of outrage, Debra returned to the typewriter, angrily erasing and correcting each mistake she'd made, desperately wishing she could as easily wipe out her mental image of the man in her carriage house. Yet it seemed she'd no sooner become embroiled in the tangled lives of the Gable, Walker and Fielding clans than the faint sounds of sawing and hammering would penetrate their world, riveting her thoughts to reality. In the end, it was Graham who saved the day by leaving as unobtrusively as he'd come.

The days slowly passed, and routine set in. Graham arrived early each morning, going straight to the carriage house. Not quite daring to tempt fate, Debra simply left a pot of fresh-brewed coffee on the kitchen counter while she saw to her own affairs. If their paths crossed, it was pure coincidence to which each reacted with appropriate nonchalance. From Debra's standpoint, Graham was fully content to invest his energy in his work. In turn, she acknowledged that a potentially volatile situation was under control. Not that she found him any less appealing as the days passed. His apparent indifference seemed to make him all the more attractive. But she kept her distance, viewing his progress in the carriage house only after he'd left for the night. This physical distance was her salvation.

By the end of the week, Graham had completed the few structural repairs the building demanded and had installed new windows, a skylight and a large thermal dome in the loft. With the simple introduction of light, he'd done wonders, removing what few reservations Debra may have initially had regarding the conversion of the carriage house into a temporary home. She began eagerly to anticipate the surprises that would await her each evening, finding in them subsequent justification for having so thoroughly trusted Graham's judgment.

Indeed, as Tuesday, Wednesday and Thursday of the second week passed, she grew impatient. Her writing kept her busy, as did various shopping expeditions and obligatory stops at the post office. But she felt an increasing urge to witness the progress as it occurred. By Friday, she gave in.

The carriage house was more quiet than she'd heard it all week. Gone were the sounds of hammer and nail, the shrill whir of the handsaw, the more subtle one of the sander. Even the door failed to whine when she pulled it open and stepped through. Graham himself seemed nowhere about. Frowning, she walked farther, reached the center of the large room, then turned.

"There you are!" she exclaimed, spotting him in the loft. "You're painting?"

He was on his hands and knees, working slowly backward from the far end. He spared her little more than a glance. "It's varnish." Then he paused and sat back on his heels. "Well, what do you think?"

Debra followed his gaze as it made a broad sweep of the loft. "I can't believe it! It's great!" Indeed, it was light and airy, its wood a naturally pale hue, now that it had been relieved of its aged veneer. "Can I come up?" she asked on impulse, her hand already reaching for the banister of the spiral staircase he'd built.

Graham didn't answer; he simply followed her progress until she reached the top and slid to the floor not far from him. "Be careful." He pointed to her side. "It's still wet."

She couldn't have moved, so absorbed was she in admiring the view she'd heretofore only seen in the dark. "You're nearly finished!" she exclaimed in amazement.

Picking up his brush, he continued to spread the varnish skillfully. His strokes were even and efficient, one meeting the other with little or no overlap. "This will protect the wood for whatever you want to do up here in the future. In the meantime, your bedroom will be that much more refined than if I'd left the boards bare."

Looking down the length of the broad loft, she could actually begin to visualize her things in place. The large brass bed would go at the far end beneath the dome, inviting her to count the stars from her pillow and awaken to the sun. The desk would fit perfectly against the sloping roof whose new skylight would let in plenty of light while she worked. In other nooks and crannies, she could stow her books, the stereo, the few small tables and easy chairs she'd brought from New York. And underneath, on the back wall of the carriage house, he'd built a wall filled with shelves to hold those other assorted crates and boxes her moving truck had delivered.

Standing now, she leaned across the waist-high balustrade to study his handiwork. Graham's sharp voice brought her quickly upright.

"Careful, Debra!"

"I'm all right."

"If you don't watch yourself, you'll tumble over." He had paused, paint brush in his hand. "Maybe I should have made the railing higher."

"Don't be silly! It's perfectly safe this way. Besides, any higher and the open line of the loft would have been destroyed. But then"—she eyed him in soft accusation—"you know that."

"Yes," he replied evenly, "I know that." With a gruff twist, he set to work once more.

Debra felt as though she'd been dismissed, yet she couldn't get herself to leave. Puzzled by his mood, she studied his tawny head, downcast now in concentration on his task. He was a loner; she accepted that. In the two weeks that he'd been working for her, he'd never once brought in a helper. Perhaps she distracted him. More probably, she annoyed him. Leaning silently against the railing, she came to the discouraging conclusion that though he might find her physically appealing, he simply didn't like her.

Feeling oddly deflated, she wound her way down the staircase, turned a last time to admire the scene he'd created, then left him in peace. She'd no sooner set foot inside the kitchen than the phone rang. The timing was perfect; she needed a boost. She dashed through to the living room and lifted the receiver to her ear.

"Hello?"

The faintest sound of static tipped her off. "Hi, doll." It was Harris. "How's it going?"

"Fine, Harris," she responded enthusiastically. Then, with a bit more caution as she settled cross-legged onto the floor, she asked, "Did you get my package?"

"Came in last night. It looks good, Deb."

When he'd called three days before, they'd discussed the content of that script; she hadn't anticipated a problem. There had to have been another reason for his call. "How was the meeting this morning?" she asked.

"We missed you." His voice hung heavy, as if he half-expected that she'd rectify things by agreeing to rush back.

She simply smiled patiently. "Thanks, Harris. How is everyone?"

"They're all fine. Kept asking about you."

"Then I'm glad you and I are in such close touch," she teased, unwilling to give an inch. "You can reassure them I'm well. So . . . what's the latest?"

She listened as Harris, accepting defeat graciously, proceeded to preview the outlines he'd be sending, to clue her in as to the general direction of the show for the next month's worth of scripts. There was nothing outlandish; to her relief, even the incest theme had slipped into the shadows. Only when he came to the Gable line, one that she'd been instrumental in introducing to the show, did Debra's eyes darken.

"But Harris, we've discussed that before. Selena has run away so often, and she *always* comes meekly back with Jonathan. The women of America must be dying!"

"She's been gone for weeks this time. That's longer than she's ever before managed to evade Jonathan."

Debra's laugh was soft and indulgent. "You and I both know that Marjorie wanted the time off. Playing Selena Gable day after day must grow tedious, particularly for a woman as spirited as Marjorie. I say we bring her back with a bang."

"What you're saying is that we *shouldn't* bring her back, that we should have her stamp her foot and refuse to budge."

"Not at all. I think Selena should finally stand up for herself. Her continual leaving and returning is boring. Let's give her some backbone. If she left Jonathan because she suspects he's been cheating on her again, let's have her threaten something in turn."

"It's not as simple as that, Deb. Jonathan has that small fact of Ben's parentage to hold over Selena."

"And she has her father's political clout. So they're even. I say we play on Selena's intelligence."

"She's not intelligent!" Harris protested. "She's never been intelligent!"

But Debra held out a hand. "Now that's not true. She's certainly kept Jonathan over a barrel dangling those government contracts in front of him. Let's have her call his bluff."

"You mean, threaten him with losing the contracts? But that would harm her, too. Her own children have as much of an investment in Gable Electronics as Jonathan does."

"True. But there's the other side of the issue. The children—at least Adam and Cynthia—are Jonathan's flesh and blood, too. I think he'll be reluctant to jeopardize their future." With the phone cradled between jaw and shoulder, she leaned forward to stoke the fire. Then she settled back, facing it.

"So?"

"So," she resumed, her voice growing firmer, "when Jonathan finally locates Selena, they have a terrific argument. For the first time, Selena really resists his meaningless words of reconciliation. For the first time, she throws it all back at him—her opinions, her feelings. I'm telling you, our female viewers will stand up cheering."

"The guys are gonna love this," came the distant grumble, the "guys" being Debra's fellow writers.

"You can handle them, Harris. Besides, I've always told you, you should have more female writers. Tell the guys that Jonathan will have his day somewhere on down the road. For now, let's give Selena a chance."

Harris's sigh easily skimmed the distance from New York to New Hampshire. "Okay, doll. What's the clincher?"

A mischievous grin played over Debra's lips. "Selena can very coyly inform Jonathan that she's been in touch with Rachel Lowden."

"Rachel Lowden? She's been out of the story for nearly five months."

"Well, we'll bring her back . . . at least, we'll bring in the threat of her return . . . of her very *pregnant* return."

There was a long pause. Then Harris lowered his voice playfully. "You're very evil, Debra. Do you know that?"

"It's a prerequisite for the job, isn't it?" she mused more sadly, thinking of the same "evil" in her colleagues. Jason had taken it one step further; had that been inevitable?

"And what will Selena do when Jonathan corners her about Ben?"

Debra tipped up her chin. "Jonathan has no proof. Selena knows that. When Richard had his stroke two years ago, the only possible testimony to Ben's extramarital conception was sealed into silence with him. If, at some future point, we want to give him a miraculous recovery, we can. In fact, it could even relate to the implant research Adam has just committed the company to. Now that I think of it, that would be Jonathan's counterrevenge."

"Not bad."

"It'll be fine, Harris—as long as Selena has her day." She was determined to make her point. "It's wrong that Jonathan carries on so. Sure, this time it's a false alarm, but for God's sake, the guy has had one torrid affair after another!" Her voice rose in vehemence. "Somehow things don't seem even; there's no justice. For what Selena did just once, she's continually punished. Jonathan has done the same thing repeatedly, and he suffers nothing more than a little embarrassment, a little annoyance when his wife runs away."

"The guys are *really* gonna love this," Harris murmured in distant echo of himself. But if he sounded intimidated, it was all for show; as story editor, not to mention producer, his power was supreme.

Eyes blazing, reflecting the fire, Debra argued on. 'If the guys can't cope, that's *their* problem. These are modern times. A woman has a right to stand up for what she wants even if that happens to be nothing more than a little respect from her husband! And if she can't get that, maybe she can be excused for conniving here and there." During the time she paused for a fast breath, she had an idea. "If I had the courage, I'd slip Selena a younger man, a gorgeous hunk who'd worship her. Hell, if I had the courage, I'd find one myself. Not necessarily younger. But certainly caring and affectionate." Her eyes narrowed, her voice sharpened. "And so smitten that he would gladly overlook my past."

"It's certainly a lurid one," Harris teased, tongue in cheek.

She had, of course, been thinking of Selena and the brief affair that had produced Ben. But Harris's quip deserved recognition. "Lurid is one word for it," she drawled facetiously, then grew alert when something caught her eye, the merest movement reflected in the brass handle of the poker resting against the fireplace. Spinning around, she found Graham glaring at her and immediately lowered her voice.

"Uh, Harris, I've really got to run."

"And leave me up in the air after that outburst? Boy, you're really angry, aren't you?"

"What do you mean?"

"With Jason. Listen, for what it's worth, it's over."

"That's what I've been trying to tell everyone."

"No, I mean his thing with Jackie."

Aware of Graham's presence, Debra turned back to the fire and lowered her voice. "I really don't care."

"He still loves you."

"Harris," she vowed tersely, "that's just not true."

"He does, Deb."

"Harris . . ." she warned, stifling the urge to glance over her shoulder. "Listen, let me know what you decide to do with Selena's thing. How about if I talk with you next week. Okay?"

There was a pause, then a resigned "Fine, doll."

"And Harris?"

"Uh-huh?"

She smiled. "Cheer up. As soon as he finds someone else, he'll get off your back." She'd read the situation correctly.

"Damn, but I hope so. . . . Bye, Deb."

As though spent by her recent tirade, she replaced the phone gently. Then she twisted around to look up at Graham. "I'm sorry. I couldn't seem to get him off. Did you . . . want to use the phone?"

Graham's voice was a taut rumble. "Would you really do that . . . take up with someone simply to spite your husband?" In the grimness of his expression, she saw abundant disdain.

"I don't have a husband," she replied quietly.

"All right. Ex-husband. Would you launch into an affair to spite him?" Gone was his earlier indifference. The eyes that probed her were sharp and relentless.

"You shouldn't have eavesdropped."

"But I did. And now you're evading my question."

Knowing she was and not quite knowing why, Debra fought to keep her voice low and even. "I don't owe you an answer."

His lips twisted sardonically. "Then . . . I guess that's it."

"What?"

His jaw tensed. "A very subtle admission of guilt."

She couldn't believe it. "As seen only in the mind of a hopeless chauvinist! Graham, I'm surprised at you! I mean, I know that you folks up here are a tad more conservative than us city folk, but . . . really! You're in no position to make judgments about my morals. You know nothing about them!" Hurt and angry, she jumped to her feet and reached for her jacket. "I'm going out!" she stated as she shoved her arms into its sleeves. "Use the phone all you want."

Her exit would have been perfect had it not been for the fact that Graham stood in her way. When she made to sidestep him, he easily blocked her move.

Burned by his closeness, she stepped back. "Excuse me. I'd like to leave now."

"Would you do it, Debra?"

"Go out? You bet. I've been meaning to get to the supermarket all week."

It wasn't what he'd meant, and she knew it. The darkness of his expression, the smoldering of his eyes, told her as much. As she looked up, her heart faltered.

"Would you use yourself that way?" he growled.

"I want to go, Graham. Please move."

He shook his head slowly, then narrowed his gaze. "I've been trying to be noble, trying to leave you alone. But if it's a question of me or some other clod—"

It took Debra a minute to follow. When she did, she was incensed. "Are you kidding? I'd never—"

"Never take up with your carpenter?" He took a step closer. "I seem to recall a reaction once. You liked it when I touched you." When his hand moved forward to remind her of that day in the carriage house, she deftly snaked around him. But as quickly he shot an arm out to snag her waist. "Don't run now," he crooned derisively. "Things are getting interesting." His arm tightened.

"Let me go," she cried, all too aware of the strength of that arm, of the strength of the entire body whose side touched hers. But his response was to drag her around until her back was flush against his chest. To her infinite dismay, her eyes settled on the bed, and she wondered in a moment of panic what had ever possessed her to leave it in the living room.

"You can't do this, Graham," she gasped when his other arm stole inside her jacket to take possession of her ribs.

His breath warmed her ear. "Why not? It'd feel good. You know, relieve that tension."

"I'm not tense. Graham . . . stop!" His teeth bit lightly into her lobe; at her cry, he slid his lips to her neck. She tried to pry his arms away, but they might have been steel bands for all the success she had.

"You smell good, babe—"

"Don't 'babe' me! It's demeaning!" His tongue moved in warm, soft ways along the sensitive cord of her neck. "Graham," she begged in a whisper. "Don't!"

For a split second, she thought she might have penetrated his haze of passion. With a final kiss, he lifted his lips from her neck and slowly turned her in his arms. But his embrace tightened before she could flee. With one arm encircling her back, he spread his hand across her throat and tipped her face up with his thumb and forefinger.

Debra had never seen pure lust before, but she knew just what it was upon encountering his gaze. Graham wanted her; he had every intention of taking her. By rights, she should have been frightened. The only thing that frightened her, though, was the insidious weakness in her knees—that and the knowledge that for the sake of her own self-respect, she'd have to fight him.

"There, now," he growled, his voice thick. "You've hired the right man."

"I'll fire you!" she threatened, but he only tipped his head back and laughed. His neck was firm and sinewed, his jaw long and straight, his teeth a healthy flash of white.

"You won't do that." He eyed her with confidence.

All humor suddenly vanished, leaving a voice that was begrudgingly blunt. "You hooked me on your house; I hooked you on my plans. It works both ways, Debra. It's as simple as that."

He was right. In a way, they were like Selena and Jonathan, each with an irreplaceable something the other needed.

"But it'd be rape if you force me."

"I won't force you." Lowering his head, he taunted her cheek with his lips, brushing them lightly just below her eye to force her lashes down. The involuntary tremor that shook her illustrated his point. There'd be no force; he wouldn't need it.

With that realization, Debra forcefully wedged her hands between them. "Graham, let go!" she gritted, waging a battle on two fronts now. "This is ridiculous! You won't want to have to face me if you go through with this. Where would your joy be then in building my house?"

His lips were a breath from her own, his voice deep and sensual. "It would be in coming to wake you every morning, crawling in to share your warmth, feeling your body mold itself to mine before I settle down to work. No, Debra, it wouldn't bother me at all! You're attractive and available"—his hand pressed lower— "and you do something indecent to every vow I've made." He seemed suddenly more angry than aroused, though the last was a hard, aching fact.

And Debra was losing the battle; her own vows seeming distant, vague. "Please," she begged, "don't do this to me! I don't know you. I don't know anything about you!"

"And you've never made love to a stranger before? Come on; where's your imagination?"

"Imagination's got nothing to do with it!" she countered in a last-ditch try for self-restraint. "For all I know, you're married or engaged or carrying on with some woman who'd be sick if she learned that you couldn't resist your employer."

The arm about her back tightened convulsively; the lips, close to her own, grew hard. "If I were married or engaged," he seethed, "I sure as hell *wouldn't* be doing what I intend to do now." Without further word, he forced her face around until their lips collided.

Chapter Five

*H*e was a carpenter, a man of brawn, a physical man above all else. If Debra had ever doubted that, his brazen kiss now proved it beyond a doubt. His lips were parted and forceful, moving hers against all resistance. Slanting ardently, they seemed to devour her with an insatiable need that took her breath away.

When he finally lifted his mouth, she felt dizzy. Her fingers clutched the wool of his shirt; her body sagged against his. She was stunned; Graham assumed she'd accepted defeat.

"That's better," he growled. "I want you pliant in my arms, pliant and giving. Women's rights have their place, but not here."

On a burst of indignation, she began to struggle. "You're a lout and a bully! Let go of me!"

His eyes scorched her moistened lips. "What? And miss the fun? I know what it is, Debra. You're one of those women who needs to put up a fight, to play the role of the wronged maiden." When she squirmed more wildly, he simply tightened his arms. "Well, there's no need for that now. I won't tell anyone if you give in and enjoy yourself."

"You—" Her angry protest was bitten off by his lips as they renewed their assault. Seconds later, though, they gentled and began to move more persuasively than imperiously. Threatened all the more, Debra held herself stiff. She was determined to deny him his satisfaction.

Graham was no less determined to achieve it. Daring to release her back, he imprisoned her head in his long fingers, his palms positioning her face as if it were a wedge of wood in a vise. "Open your mouth, Debra," he demanded, low and rasping. "Open it." Without awaiting her compliance, he began to place bold, hard kisses around the corners of her mouth, each kiss drawing her, tempting her, luring her with an odd brand of roughness.

She couldn't identify it, that oddness. It was as if his lusty display of aggression were the front for a deep, abiding need, as if his urgency were born of loneliness rather than pure biology. Beneath his force she sensed something warmer, softer. Perhaps it was his hands, so firm in their hold, yet not in the least bit hurtful. Perhaps it was the faintest tremor in his body, a tremor that spoke of attempts at control that a truly brutal man would have scorned.

His tongue hadn't yet ventured forth in lure . . . Suddenly, she wanted it to. She wanted him to taste her fully. Yes, she was curious. If his boldness stirred her senses, she wondered what his deeper probing would do. But there was more. That faint thread of desperation in him elicited a corresponding thread of compassion in her. In that split second, she wanted to fill his need, to do something for him, to be something to him.

Her lips grew less hard, then softer, finally submitting to his pressure and parting to his. But when his tongue surged through, he was the marauder once more, sweeping the dark interior of her mouth as if to know it all before she demurred. And demur she did, reacting to his invasion with renewed resistance, pushing at his chest, trying to strain away. It was wrong, she told herself, all wrong, yet when he more gently nibbled at the inside of her lips, she felt a flow of fire that threatened to consume her from within.

"Please, don't!" she cried weakly when he shifted his lips to explore the sculpted line of her cheek. "Don't . . ." But her hands clung to his shoulders, finding raw appeal in their muscularity. He'd be a good lover, bold and strong, she told herself, then began to shiver under the chill of a rising need. "No!" she cried in self-command, and inched her body away.

To her surprise, Graham allowed it. To her instant chagrin, she understood why. With but the slightest forward move on his part and another backing away on hers, she was up against the bed. Before she could react, he had slipped his arm down under her bottom and lifted her off her feet. By the time she caught her breath, she was on her back, looking up into a face that was as taut with desire as was the body that settled beside her.

"What are you *doing?*" She gasped and turned, only to find her thighs captured by his leg, her shoulders by his hands.

He didn't speak, simply lowered his head and kissed her with the same raging fire she felt inside. At least he was honest, she mused. He wanted her; he didn't play at the chase as those other men she'd known had done. Oh, she'd always been faithful to Jason. But there had been men who had approached her, whispering suggestive nothings in her ear, pussyfooting around without the guts simply to ask her to bed. Perhaps they'd not had the courage, knowing she'd refuse. But there *was* something exciting about a man who knew what he wanted and set out to take it.

Was she as honest, she wondered as her lips responded in helpless answer to his provocation? He tasted good—his mouth, his tongue, even his teeth as she ran the tip of her tongue along their edge. He even smelled good—the smell of work, of distant varnish, of fresh wood, of sweat. Oh, yes, she wanted to respond. But could she be as frank about this physical craving he'd inspired? Could she let him have his way . . . then live with herself tomorrow?

"Graham!" She gasped when he pushed her hair aside and lowered his lips to sample the curve of her neck. "Enough!"

"No, love," he crooned as he touched her gently. "I don't think I can ever get enough. You have no idea what you do to me!" The last was an admission torn from him. In it, Debra felt the spark of her own power. She'd somehow disappointed Jason so that he'd sought satisfaction with another woman. Knowing how deeply she stirred this man—this exceedingly virile, earthy man—had to be a compliment to her femininity.

"Tell me what I do," she commanded, threading her fingers through the lushness of his hair and forcing his eyes to meet hers. "Tell me, Graham."

But he wanted no part of word games. Levering himself more fully atop her, he vividly demonstrated her effect. Then, with his forearms bearing the brunt of his weight, he strung a fiery path of kisses from her chin, down her neck, to that pale hollow of her throat.

Closing her eyes, Debra savored every sensation to the fullest, not only that erotic pressure of his lips against her skin but also the heady weight of his man's body with its long, lean lines and its overwhelming hardness. There remained a force about him, but it was tethered now, aimed at eliciting the response he craved.

And it did. Debra felt as though she were burning, as though her only salvation lay in twisting beneath him, in using his body to smother the flame. She was barely aware of the play of his hands until she felt a waft of cool air on her chest and realized that her blouse had been unbuttoned and now lay pushed open. Whether her gasp was of dismay or a chill, she didn't know. Nor did she have time to wonder. For Graham's hands proceeded to warm her while his lips kept hers occupied.

He touched her with the skill of a carpenter, a carpenter most skilled as a man. His hardened palms skimmed her ribs; his agile fingers slid across her bra's lacy cup. Again, she was enticed by the contrast in him, the roughened feel of his skin working with such sensual finesse. This was no workman limited to framing a house; he could do the smallest detail work every bit as well.

When his fingers slid around the swell of her breast, she arched closer, ironically craving the force he'd shown earlier. But it wasn't to be. With agonizing gentleness, he slipped a finger under the lace of her bra, let it sizzle over the swelling fullness of her flesh to the turgid nub of her breast and rubbed slowly.

"Graham . . . oh, yes . . ."

When he kissed her, she met the greedy thrust of his tongue with her own, mindless of the gasping breath they shared in fevered syncopation. He'd been right; it *was* good. She felt warm and wanted, utterly feminine and desirable.

"Yes," she murmured, signaling her final surrender by raising her arms to his ribs, then pressing them against his back where they explored his strength as they pressed him closer. "Oh, yes, Graham . . ."

"Tell me . . ."

"It feels so . . . good." Hers was an aching moan, escaped from lips that turned to seek his.

But he drew back. His hand ceased its sweet torment, and he held himself higher, propping himself on his fists to loom over her. "You *are* a conniving one," he growled, his voice bearing far more than passion, "luring me to this job with that tempting little body of yours."

Fighting a daze of desire, Debra forced her eyes

open. "What?" she whispered, feeling she must surely have missed the start of the conversation.

Graham's face was hard. His chest labored as he tried to control himself. "I may not be that younger man, that 'gorgeous hunk' you'd give Selena," he gritted, "but damn it, I want you."

"What . . . what are you talking about?"

"We're good at making bargains. I do your house; you pay me. You keep your bed warm for me; I'll gladly overlook that lurid past of yours."

Throwing off the last of her grogginess, she eyed him in disbelief. "My . . . lurid past? There's no lurid past!"

"It's all right." He slanted her a harsh grin. "I won't question you on it. I accept you for what you are . . . as long as you do it beneath me."

"Graham," she exclaimed angrily, "you don't know what you're talking about!"

"I know enough," he countered, moving his lower body ever so subtly against hers. "This is what matters between us. Just this. Nothing more."

He'd underestimated her. With an explosion of strength born of fury, she shoved him hard, wedging just enough space to shimmy from under him and jump off the bed. "You bastard!" she cried, clutching the front of her blouse together. She felt suddenly cheap. "I don't have any *lurid* past, any more than I'd take up with one man to spite another. You've eavesdropped on a private conversation and . . . and you're way off base!" Trembling with anger, she could do nothing more than glare as Graham slowly rose from the bed and came to stand before her. His eyes were dark and remarkably cool, given the ruddy flush that lingered high on his cheeks.

"Then you correct me," he ordered in a voice that brooked no argument. Hooking one thumb through his belt loop, he let his other hand hang by his hip.

Debra glanced up at him indignantly. "I've already told you enough. I have nothing further to—"

"I'd like to know where you get this sudden streak of morality. I mean"—his tone was one of derision—"phone calls from Harris and Mike and Jason. Giving Selena a younger man to play with. Taking up with some poor adoring fool yourself. Explain!"

"You don't deserve—"

"Explain!" he thundered, grabbing her shoulders with the suddenness of the lion attacking his prey.

"You're my carpenter," she countered weakly, wishing to hurt as he had. "Nothing but my carpenter, for God's sake! I don't owe—"

"I'm a man," he seethed. "And you're playing a dangerous game. This particular carpenter may not be stupid, but he's getting pretty damned impatient."

Debra had hit her mark; she'd never seen him quite as angry. The tautness of his jaw was nearly as forbidding as the amber shards of his eyes were cutting. Even through her jacket, the pressure of his fingers bit into her flesh. Had she not been frantically clutching at her blouse, she would have reached up in an effort to relieve the pain.

"You want explanations?" she asked, eying him with a last bit of boldness. "Then you'll get them." She took a steadying breath. "Harris is my story editor. Mike is my half-brother. Jason is my ex-husband and fellow writer. Selena," she spit, "happens to be a character *I* created. And if I want to find her a younger man, a warm, adoring, gentle man, *I will!*"

Breathlessly, she endured Graham's appalled stare. Very slowly, he eased the force of his fingers. Then he knit his brows in concern and spoke more gently, with hesitance. "Are you . . . under treatment now?"

"Under treatment?"

"Are you seeing a psychiatrist?"

"Why in the world would I want to do that?"

His expression was one of deep compassion, his words slow and cautious. "You know what schizophrenia is, don't you, Debra?"

At first, she didn't understand. "Schizophrenia?" she echoed, a blank look on her face. Then his implication became clear, and her eyes widened. "Schizophrenia?" she exclaimed hysterically. Heedless of the state of her blouse, she brought both arms up to push him away. "I'm not schizophrenic!" she cried. "Selena is a *character*—one of *many* I write about every day of the week." Taking a step back, she pointed a shaky finger toward where her set lay innocuously on the floor. "I'm a scriptwriter! I write for television—for soap opera! Why do you *think* I watch that show so faithfully every day? I *write* for it, damn it! *Write!*"

Graham stood in stunned silence, towering above her, yet soundly humbled. Unable to deal with the scope of his misconception, he simply watched Debra whirl around and head for the door. With its slamming, he frowned, hung his head and rubbed the taut muscles of his neck, then looked questioningly back up. But she'd gone. Even now he heard the rev of her motor as she sped from the house. He wanted to tell her to be careful . . . even to make sure she buttoned her blouse. But, then, she was a big girl. A sophisticated woman. A woman with a career . . . and an impressive one at that. Who was he to tell her *anything* after the blunder he'd made?

With the onset of slow-creeping mortification, he backed blindly to the bed and sank down on its edge. He'd thought himself an intelligent man, yet here he'd totally misjudged things. For an instant, he had half-assumed her to be mentally unstable. Lord knows she wouldn't have been the first to have left the city on the verge of a nervous breakdown. But . . . Debra? Looking to the ceiling in self-disgust, he gritted his teeth. How could he have thought it even for that instant when all along she'd struck him as being totally rational and collected.

When he lowered his head, his eye fell on her typewriter. She was a scriptwriter—so much for the idle woman who needed her dose of soap to make it through the day! No wonder she'd been insistent on watching her program that first day. She'd written the script, for God's sake! Of course, she'd want—no, *need*—to watch. He could imagine the importance of keeping that continuity.

Fingers gripping the edge of the pale-blue spread, he thought about what he'd done. He honestly had thought her some kind of swinger, what with the string of men who'd called. And then, when he'd heard her on the phone this morning . . . she *had* sounded slightly immoral. How was he to know? Damn it, why hadn't she told him the truth from the start?

A grimace thinned his lips as he realized she'd probably enjoyed her little joke. Oh, yes, despite the respect he might have now for her talent as a writer, she was still a city girl, slick and conniving. That part *had* been true, he thought, and raked a hand through his hair. She had managed to captivate him from the start, even against his will. Fitting, then, that he should have sought to take her against her will today. But it *hadn't* been against her will, had it? She had strained toward him, had cried his name at the end. She wouldn't have fought him had he staked his claim. But what after? How *many* times had he asked himself this same question?

Pushing angrily away from the bed, he stalked to the window and stared at the driveway. His brown pickup seemed lonely without her Blazer for company. He looked down at his wrist to check the time, only to recall that he didn't wear a watch. Not anymore. He hadn't since he'd moved here. It was one of the things he loved about life in the country—time, lots of time.

New York, on the other hand, ran on schedule. There a watch had been a necessity. His day had been a marathon from one appointment to the next, with work at the drafting board stolen like an orange slice greedily sucked on the run. Absently stroking that naked wrist, he tried to remember the last time he'd inadvertently looked for his watch. It had been a long, long time ago.

His eyes clung to the road leading back up the drive, yet there was no sign of the Blazer's return. Twisting his head, he scanned the room for a sign of the time, finally spying the clock radio practically hidden on the floor by the bed. It was one o'clock. She'd be back soon. After all, her show began in thirty minutes.

Softly cursing his stupidity, he stalked back through the kitchen, grabbed a Mountain Dew from the refrigerator and returned to the carriage house. This was where he belonged, he decided. A workman, sticking to his trade. He'd blown it with Debra. It seemed that he'd simply lost touch with the faster world since he'd dropped out. Eight years. A long time to be out of the mainstream. It had never bothered him before. Why now?

Tipping the can, he savored the cool fizz of soda as it trickled down his throat. Then, walking to his truck, he settled himself in the driver's seat with the door open, reached for the brown bag that had waited patiently in the shade on the floor and lit into the first of the two ham and cheese sandwiches he'd packed before he'd left home. Ham and cheese . . . he looked down at the drab combination. Debra wouldn't eat ham and cheese. She'd undoubtedly munch on a salad, a piece of quiche or a pint of yogurt. He knew the type—skin and bones for the sake of vanity. But . . . she wasn't skin and bones, was she? He'd felt her body and knew differently. Though slender, she was soft and delicately curved. And when she'd swollen to his touch—

Shifting abruptly in his seat, he wolfed down two

bites of sandwich in succession, nearly choked, found salvation in another swig of soda. She'd remembered. Mountain Dew. *Who was she,* damn it, and what was she doing threatening his peace of mind?

The soda and sandwiches were long since gone, and still he had no answers. Returning to the carriage house, he set to work installing the locks he had purchased. He'd barely drilled a hole, though, when he put down his tools and went into the house. Without quite realizing his own intent, he found himself setting up the small television and turning it on. "Love Games" was well underway. Sinking down on the floor with his back against the bed, he watched intently. By the time the last scene had faded from the screen, he believed it all. Yes, Selena was a character, albeit only referred to by others today. Harris Ward was listed as a producer, Jason Barry as a member of the writing staff. The appearance of Debra's name was almost anticlimactic.

With the set stowed once more in its case, he resumed work on the lock in the carriage-house door, inserting screws with the force of his frustration, then looking around for something to hit.

What a fool he'd been . . . and how badly he'd treated Debra! Sure, she might not be his type, but she did deserve some measure of respect! If only he could fault her capitulation in his arms, but he couldn't. That physical spark existed despite any other differences they might have. Hell, hadn't he broken his own vows to avoid her? Hadn't he been the one to initiate that ill-fated romp? Much as he would have liked to believe that he'd simply reacted to her in anger, in truth there was more. He *was* attracted to her. And, damn it, he didn't know what to do about it!

Grabbing an ax, he stormed from the carriage house and attacked an old dead tree in the yard. He'd had time to hack off no more than the lower limbs when the sound of a motor caught his ear. Glancing briefly toward the road, he saw the Blazer turn slowly into the drive. When Debra finally drew to a stop, he was back chopping in long, forceful strokes.

Killing the motor, she sat for a minute wondering what to say, what to do. She owed him an apology; she should have told him sooner. She'd thought it a kind of game, and it had backfired. How could she hold him responsible? And as for the way she'd melted toward him in the end . . . why, he'd almost be justified in believing the worst about her. What kind of woman arrived in an isolated spot and proceeded to hand-pick the tallest, most muscular, most extraordinarily virile man to work for her? Granted, this one was a brilliant designer and a skillful craftsman as well. But the scenario sounded hauntingly familiar. She'd written variations on its theme any number of times!

Shaking her head, she slid from the Blazer and headed for the house, deep in thought. She wouldn't have seen Graham if he had looked up; he didn't. For that matter, she wouldn't have known what to say if he'd spoken; he didn't. Once inside, she tossed her jacket on the bed and went directly through to the kitchen to make a cup of tea. Its warmth did little to ease her inner chill.

She'd been driving ever since she'd left the house. Actually, she'd spent part of the time pulled up on the shoulder of a quiet road overlooking a pasture. And she'd thought of Graham. Yes, she regretted having been less than truthful from the start. And yes, she was embarrassed by the way she'd begged for him at the end. But her greatest cause for self-reproach was in the way she'd put him down.

It had been arrogant—and unnecessary. What she'd meant when she'd so crudely called him "nothing but my carpenter" was that they were nothing but two people crossing paths for the sake of a temporary goal.

What her words had implied, however—and in her anger she had allowed them to imply—was that he was somehow inferior to her.

It wasn't true. As a carpenter, he possessed skills she couldn't hope to imitate. The blueprints he'd drawn for her rivaled any she'd ever seen, both for technical excellence and vision. Indeed, there were things about him, other things, that suggested he was well educated. His speech was cultured, his vocabulary complex, even his sense of humor carried an undercurrent of sophistication.

Wandering toward the front of the house, she paused at the window of the empty dining room. Firewood. He was chopping that dead tree into firewood. Entranced, she watched him swing the ax in a near-complete circle, drawing it back and up by his leg, then higher to his chest and shoulder, then above and more . . . until he put the force of his muscular build into the downward wham that neatly split the log. Releasing a breath, she sank back against the window frame and sipped her tea, which seemed suddenly cool.

He intrigued her. He had from the first when he had so vehemently rejected her job offer. Yes, she'd been physically aware of him. But there was more. Perhaps it was simply habit. After all, writing about people, their actions and motivations, was her business.

Her head shot up, and she straightened. "Love Games"! She'd completely forgotten! Casting a frantic glance at her watch, she realized she'd missed it completely. Twice now he'd made her miss it. Twice! Irked at her preoccupation with a man who was nothing more than a passing figure in her life, she stormed into the living room and propped herself before the typewriter. It was there that Graham found her when, half an hour later, he entered the house.

Arms piled high with newly chopped wood, he spared her a fleeting glance as he made his way to the fireplace. Squatting to lay the logs one by one in a nearby basket, he darted her another look. Debra sat still, returning his gaze.

"Did you get to the market?" he asked as though he were simply passing the time of day.

"Uh . . . no," she answered softly. She'd completely forgotten that, too. "I took a drive. There . . . wasn't much traffic." Dumb, she thought. This isn't New York.

He simply nodded and turned his attention back to the logs. "There rarely is. It's sometimes worse in the fall when the tourists come up to see the foliage. It gets beautiful then."

"It's beautiful now."

"True." Finishing his task, he stood and brushed his hands together. "There. That should hold you for a while. I'll keep working on the tree. It would have had to come down, anyway."

"I know. And . . . thank you."

Avoiding her eyes, he nodded again, then turned to leave. When he paused, dipped his chin to his chest and reached up to rub his neck, she held her breath.

"Listen, Debra," he began, looking gently down at her. "I'm sorry about before. I jumped to several wrong conclusions. It shouldn't have happened."

Debra listened to his apology but shook her head at its end. "No, Graham, *I'm* the one at fault. I should have told you about my work that first day when you caught me watching the show. As for Harris and Mike and Jason"—she grinned more sheepishly—"I guess I should have been more specific when I mentioned their names to you. No wonder you got the wrong idea. And what with the conversation you overheard today, well, it *must* have sounded bizarre!"

A tawny brow arched beneath his hair. "Bizarre is one word for it. I'd begun to imagine you were thinking of turning this house"—his eye skimmed the room, imagining it as it would soon be—"*my masterpiece*, into a den of iniquity." The slightest twitch at the corner of his lips spoke of his returning humor. Debra felt a weight lift from her shoulders.

"No," she said with a sigh, "the house is mine, for me alone. I may have house guests once in a while, but I'm hoping to find peace and quiet here."

"You will. . . . I have."

It seemed the perfect opening. "How long have you been here?" she asked, reaching the sudden conclusion that he wasn't a native of the state.

"Eight years. I've been lucky. There's been more than enough business to keep me going. As for the tranquility up here," he said, smiling, "that could keep me going forever."

Debra tucked her legs more comfortably beneath her and leaned back against the wall. "I know what you mean. There's something about the quiet, about the sound of the birds in the morning—"

"You haven't even heard much of that yet. Give it another few weeks until more of the birds are back and the mating season gets underway . . ." His voice trailed off into a silently shared awkwardness. "Well . . . anyway . . . it's nice."

She smiled softly, then nodded. "I'm looking forward to it."

Buoyed by her smile, Graham spoke gently. "You missed your program."

She blushed. "I know."

"I watched."

Her eyes brightened. "You did?"

"Uh-huh. I missed the beginning, but the rest held me riveted to the set."

"Come on, Graham," she chided, eying him askance.

He held up a placating hand. "Okay. So I wasn't riveted. Not to the story itself, at any rate. But I was fascinated with the dialogue and the fact that you wrote it—"

"Not today's show. I think it would have been Don's."

"But still, your name was listed with the credits. You must be very talented."

She minimized the accomplishment with a shrug. "I work hard, but I enjoy it."

"Have you been doing it for long?"

"Six years."

"Then you were very young when you started. I would have thought it would be tough to break into a field like that."

"It is. I had . . . a little help."

"Don't tell me. Your dad is a network bigwig."

"Not quite."

"Then . . . your mother must be an actress, one of the regulars."

"Nope."

"Then . . . it's got to be Jason." He cocked his head by way of adding a question mark.

"Yes." She smiled with poignance. "Jason. I met him at a writer's workshop when I was a senior in college. He was giving a seminar—he wrote for another soap at the time. We started dating, got married. Among other things, he taught me the trade."

"Either he was a good teacher . . . or you had the aptitude for it all along."

"A little of both, I guess," she mused aloud. "I was an English major and had my heart set on writing the great American novel one day." The last was drawled with abundant self-mockery. "Jason's seminar was really my first introduction to scriptwriting. It fascinated me. Between the writing itself and Jason's way with words, I was enthralled."

"With Jason?"

"With him, too." Her gaze fell to her lap, where her

fingers lay long, slender and bare; then she sighed. "Anyway"—she looked up—"I started working with him on the side. You know, writing a scene here and there when he was short on time."

"You collaborated."

"Unofficially, at first."

Graham's eyes darkened. "You mean, he took all the credit?"

"Oh, it wasn't like that." She jumped quickly to Jason's defense. "After all, we were married by that time, and he was supporting me, anyway. I didn't want the credit or the money. It would simply have shifted from one pocket to the other."

"That was a beneficent attitude. Most people would insist on the limelight."

"I don't like the limelight."

He eyed her skeptically. "Really? But . . . wait. We're getting off the track. I want to hear the rest of the story." He stood with his legs planted in a comfortable stance, his hands in his back pockets. Debra wondered if he wished to sit, but vetoed suggesting it for fear he'd interpret the gesture as a come-on. Given the earlier fiasco, she was gun-shy.

"There's not that much more to tell," she said. "When it got to the point where I was writing full days' scripts, Jason insisted on informing the producers that I was as capable as he was. Not that it was true, but it gave them the leeway to release one of the other writers who'd been wanting out. And I was in. That's it."

"You're too modest," Graham chided, eying her more narrowly. "Show business can be cruel, from what I've heard. You have to be good to get in, either with or without connections. Who's to say your work isn't *better* than Jason's?"

"I am. He's good. His ideas are consistent, and his flow is always that little bit smoother than the rest of ours." She grew pensive. "I guess you go through stages. When you start writing, you want nothing more than to fit into the mold. In this line of work, that's necessary. With six, seven, sometimes eight writers preparing successive days' worth of script, it would be disastrous if each went his own way. The viewer would be totally disconcerted. There is some freedom, though, in things like the balancing of dialogue among characters, even in interpreting characters' reactions to events. But it takes a while until you have the confidence *and* the stature to be able to enjoy that freedom."

"You don't believe you've reached that stage?"

Recalling the morning's call from Harris, Debra spoke with conviction. "I think I'm finally beginning to get there. At least, I hope so. When I watch the show now, I know immediately whose work it is. Don, Martin, Steve—each has a subtle style of his own. For the longest time, my work imitated Jason's. I hope that's changing now."

For a while, neither spoke. When Graham finally broke the silence, it was with care. "You don't sound bitter."

She looked down, then up. "About Jason?" He nodded. Tossing her hair back from her face, she shrugged. "There's nothing to be bitter about. Jason was a wonderful teacher. He's given me a career and a means to support myself. Without him, I'd never be where I am today."

"In every respect? If it weren't for Jason, wouldn't you still be back in New York?"

Pondering his question, she ran her finger along the bottom row of keys. "Yes. I guess I would. But only because Jason loved the city. I'd wanted to move for years."

"Was that . . . one of the problems?"

"In our marriage? Good God, no!" She laughed softly. "I doubt that Jason even realized how I felt, and

I wasn't about to make it an issue. He was happy; therefore, I was happy."

Graham smirked. "What a lovely arrangement."

"But it was!" Debra exclaimed, seeking to counter his sarcasm. "I mean, we had five good years. He was good to me. We led a very active life—lots of parties and all—and we were successful."

"What happened, then?"

She hadn't expected his bluntness. Looking down again, she frowned. Somehow she couldn't get herself to voice the full truth. It was too humiliating. "Oh . . . I guess we just needed a break from each other. Kind of went in different directions."

"All of a sudden?"

She kept her eyes averted. "Uh-huh."

"That's strange. Really sad. It sounds like you and Jason had something good going. To simply . . . need a break all of a sudden . . . it doesn't bode well for all those other supposedly happy marriages, does it?"

It took no more than a brief glance his way for Debra to realize she'd been baited. He didn't believe for a minute that Jason and she had just drifted apart. But then, why would he? People invariably assumed that to be a successful television scriptwriter was to have made it and that to have made it was to live a glossy, fast-paced life. She and Jason wouldn't just *decide* to split for the fun of it. No, there would have to be some major, dramatic conflict.

Indeed, there had been. But Debra didn't want to go into all that.

"I suppose we had our problems just like other couples," she offered by way of appeasement.

"But you loved him?"

"Yes. I did. For a while, I positively worshiped him. When we were first married, I thought he could walk on water. He seemed to know everything and everyone. Maybe . . . maybe I just couldn't keep up."

Graham sent her a punishing glance. "I don't believe that for a minute. Could it have been the other way around?" At her puzzlement, he elaborated. "Could it have been that you grew to be a threat?"

"Of course not! I had nothing on him."

"You may not have thought so, but he may have had his own insecurities."

For a moment, she pondered the possibility. Then she shook her head vigorously. "No. Jason was totally secure. He knew who he was and what he wanted." Her own words brought a wisp of pain, and the faintest shudder shook her. He had wanted Jackie. It was as simple as that.

Graham's hands were quickly out of his pockets, and he moved toward the fireplace. "It *is* getting cool in here." Hunkering down, he covered the last night's ashes with fresh logs, reached to the mantel for a long wooden match and lit the fire. Only when he was satisfied that the logs had caught did he move back, and even then it was only far enough so that he didn't deflect the warmth from Debra. He didn't sit; he simply knelt with one knee on the floor and the other bracing a forearm.

Debra watched him guardedly, unsure as to how comfortable he would make himself. Not that she had something else to do; on the contrary, her afternoon was free. In fact, now that she thought of it, she enjoyed talking with him in spite of the subject matter. Strange . . . she hadn't been able to think of Jason, to talk of him as freely, since she'd learned of his betrayal.

On her brain wave, Graham asked, "Is it difficult for you—continuing to work with him?"

"Distance does wonders," she mused, smiling gently. "I don't have to deal with Jason directly. The closest I get to him now is watching his work on the show."

"Aren't there staff meetings or something?"

"Maybe, once in a while."

"You could fly back for them . . ."

"I don't want to! And there's really no need. Besides, I'm . . . very happy staying right here."

He angled his head sharply. "For how long?"

"Excuse me?"

"For how long will you be happy here?" He thought of Joan. She had steadfastly refused so much as a visit to the country; her idea of a vacation was jetting to Paris or Acapulco or the islands.

Breathing in deeply, she feigned exasperation. "Here it comes again . . . Graham's song. I'm here for keeps! How can I convince you of that?"

"I hear what you say, but I still have doubts. From what you've said, your life in New York must have been very busy, very active socially. This must be quite a change. After a while, you're apt to get bored."

"And resort to keeping my carpenter from his work by talking his ear off, you mean?" The soft curve at the corner of her mouth kept her words from sounding harsh.

Graham followed her example. "Well, it could be a worry of mine. I'm just beginning a huge job. I wouldn't want to have to list 'gossiping with the lady of the house' as a delay comparable to 'waiting for the new furnace to arrive.' By the way"—he grew more pragmatic than playful—"the solar collection system I've got in mind should provide most of the hot water you'll need."

"That's great!"

"I'd still like to put in a back-up water heater, but it can be kept off most of the time."

"Sounds good." She nodded, then recalled the discussion that this bit of business had interrupted. "Listen, if I'm keeping you . . ."

"You're not. Everything is just about finished in the

121

carriage house. I've got a fellow coming first thing Monday to help me cart your stuff over there. Then I can begin here."

Smiling her pleasure, Debra sat straighter, then sighed. "Well, then, I guess you'll want to be going on home. . . . You live alone?"

"Uh-huh." He made no move to stand.

"Nearby?"

"Not far. About ten miles off in that direction." He cocked his head northward.

"Near the mountain?"

He gave a leisurely nod, obviously in no more of a rush than she was. Perhaps, she mused, he, too, enjoyed the company. Strange . . . she didn't feel threatened . . . or guilty . . .

"Have you ever been married?" When he slanted her a chiding glance, she quickly defended the question. "I've told you about me. It's only fair."

His smile was slow in coming, but a brilliant reward nonetheless. "I suppose so." The smile thinned. ". . . Yes, I was married once."

"Not up here."

"No."

Again, he made no offer to tell her where he'd come from. Twice he'd shunned that revelation. Debra could only assume that he was uncomfortable with it. Could she argue? She'd just evaded his question regarding the breakup of her own marriage. At least, with his holding something back, she felt half-justified.

"It was a long time ago?"

"Very."

"Yet you haven't remarried." She couldn't understand it. He was handsome, personable once he dropped his aura of aloofness, apparently successful at his work.

"No," he answered simply. Reaching forward, he took the poker and shifted the logs.

"Don't *you* get lonesome?" she asked.

His lips curved down. "Nah. There's plenty to do up here. I keep busy." His answer was evasive, and they both knew it. Keeping busy, having plenty to do, were quite different things from not being lonesome. Often, one kept busy solely to avoid loneliness.

While he studied the fire, Debra studied him. His profile was strong, rough-hewn, reminding her of who he was, where he'd chosen to be for eight years. She told herself that she was reading too much into his evasion, that she was imagining that his situation had been comparable to hers. But Graham hadn't necessarily come from the big city as she had. He seemed so at ease here; chances were good that he'd lived most of his life at this slower pace in some other small state, some other rural town. Of course, there was the matter of the plans he'd drawn for her. He had to have learned that skill somewhere. But then, there were excellent schools in many smaller cities. . . . Where *had* he studied? She opened her mouth to ask when the phone rang.

Graham's head turned toward the sound, but it was Debra's hand that reached to still it. "Hello?"

"How are you, Debra?"

Quickly recognizing the voice at the other end of the line, she smiled. "I'm fine, Stuart. And you?"

Her older brother had barely launched into what would most probably be a glib and lengthy response when Debra felt the force of Graham's scowl. Looking quickly up, she recoiled.

Chapter Six

𝒯he time Debra spent talking with Graham had been surprisingly pleasant, unexpectedly relaxing. When he suddenly scowled at her, she felt an instant loss. It was only as Stuart's voice ran on by her ear that understanding came.

Covering the mouthpiece of the phone and tucking it under her chin, she gave an urgent whisper. "Stuart is my older brother."

Her older brother's monologue ceased abruptly. "Who's there?" he barked, ever wary of what he didn't know.

Debra's eyes never left Graham's, sending him a look of chiding to combat his scowl. "It's the fellow who'll be doing the work on my house. We were just discussing things." Truthful enough, she mused, if slightly misleading.

"Oh." There was a pause. "Who is he?"

"His name is Graham Reid. He came highly recommended." Her gaze grew mischievous when Graham looked away. She would have elaborated in praise of the plans he'd drafted had not Stuart cut in.

"Are you alone with him?"

Gruff and distrustful, Stuart's tone rankled her. He'd always been protective of her, yet he'd blown it when

124

he might have helped. Even his theoretical conflict of interest was a poor defense for his behavior.

"I'm fine, Stuart," she gritted, then forced herself to relax. "But I interrupted you. What were you saying . . . something about mother?"

The voice at the other end of the line grew more annoyed than curt. "She called a little while ago. Have you spoken with her?"

"Not for several days."

"Wait till you hear the latest."

"I'm waiting."

Graham reached for another log, put it on the fire, then stood. Debra followed his movement, hoping he wouldn't leave. She could make it short with Stuart.

"She wants a big formal wedding this time." The words were stretched to their fullest and bore a dollop of contempt.

Her mother's desire for a big formal wedding was news to Debra, though she'd long since acknowledged her mother's eccentricity. "As in ushers and brides-maids and rose petals and flowing trains?"

"You got it! She can't do that, Debra! This is her fourth marriage, for God's sake!"

Debra took a breath in a bid for patience. "I know it's her fourth marriage."

"It's obscene."

"Not if she wants it."

"And that idiot Gardner—"

"I like Gardner."

"He wants to move her to Palm Beach. Did you know that?"

"No. But I think it's fine." Her lips curved in good humor. "Mom's old enough to handle him."

"You think so? Look what happened with Stanley."

"That wasn't her fault. She married Stanley because she adored having him by her side. He was a charming escort. How was she to know that he'd made it a well-paying occupation?"

Stuart snorted. "She *should* have known."

"Come off it, Stuart. She was in love with the guy!"

"In love? You really think so? And what about Michael?"

"Michael was different. When she married him, she was on the rebound from dad and thought she wanted a quieter, tamer man."

"I suppose she loved him, too?"

"In her way."

Graham stood leaning against the mantel, intently studying the flame he'd set blazing. Debra was aware that she was holding him up.

"Look, Stu. This isn't our business," she began in a futile attempt to end the conversation. Stuart wasn't buying it.

"She's our mother. Of course it's our business! I think it's up to us to talk some sense into her."

"That's where you're wrong. It's her life. She knows what she's doing. Right now she honestly believes she's in love with Gardner. What will be next week . . . or next month . . . no one knows."

"You're running away from it."

She felt herself growing irritated. Stuart had a way of doing that to her. "I'm not running away from anything! I just think we should leave mom alone."

"But we owe her something."

"You're right. We owe her loyalty and support. Those aren't your specialties, though, are they?"

Stuart proceeded to totally ignore the barb. "What we *owe* her is our advice."

"Our advice?" Debra cried, her eyes flashing. "Who are *we* to give her advice? My marriage just exploded in my face, and yours . . . well, you happen to be blessed with a saint of a wife who'll put up with anything short of assault and battery! When it comes right down to it,

Stuart, our advice isn't worth peanuts!" Choked up with anger, she lowered her head and lifted a hand to rub her forehead. "Listen, I've got to run," she murmured brokenly.

"You want to go to a formal wedding?"

"I'm not going to *any* wedding! I'm not there, remember?"

"It's an easy trip back. She'll want you here."

"She'll just have to understand. As a matter of fact, you can tell her. You owe me." She despised these calls, *despised* them.

"Owe you?"

"He was your best friend, Stuart! You knew all along what he was doing!" Engulfed in a wave of emotion, Debra had momentarily forgotten Graham's presence until her attention was drawn to him by the slight shifting of his leg. Glancing up with a start, she found him staring at her. Looking away again, she lowered her voice. "I'll have to call you another time, Stu. Bye." Only Graham's scrutiny kept her from slamming down the phone. With deliberate slowness, she replaced the receiver, as deliberately kept her eyes averted until she could get rid of her anger. In its place, though, came something else, an awareness of words she herself had said.

"I'm sorry," she murmured distractedly. "There was no need for you to have had to hear that."

Graham said nothing; he simply waited, assuming that if she wished to explain what he'd overheard, she would do it in her own time.

"My mother is thinking of remarrying," she began unsteadily, fidgeting with her hands, then standing abruptly and wandering to the window. "This will be her fourth. She wants it to be special." She wrapped her arms around her waist.

Coming quietly from behind, Graham leaned against the window frame to face her. "I can understand that."

"My brother can't. He wants to talk her out of it."

"Out of the big wedding . . . or the marriage itself?"

"Both . . . though why he thinks it's his business is beyond me."

"He's married himself?"

Eyes focused on the jagged evergreen skyline, she frowned. "I suppose you could call it that." Then she paused, thinking, struggling to put into words a nagging feeling. "Graham," she began with a breath, looking up at him, then back at the horizon. Releasing the breath, she dropped her gaze to the floor.

Sensing her struggle, he remained quiet. It was the first time he'd seen her so unsure of herself, and while he wanted to reach out, he didn't dare.

She didn't look up when she spoke, her voice an aching murmur. "Graham, do you ever get . . . down on yourself because you couldn't make your marriage last?"

He saw her pain when she slowly raised her eyes, and he understood that her upset related only indirectly to her mother and brother. If her words were an indication of where her mind was, she'd sought sympathy from the best source.

"Often," he replied quietly. "Very often."

"Even after all this time? It doesn't pass?"

He took a minute to think back to the feelings he'd had at the time of the divorce and since. "I think the sense of failure comes last. At least it did for me. At the start, there was anger and frustration. Only later, when those died down, did I get this terrible sense of inadequacy. I still feel it at times." His thoughts were on Jessie and his total inability to reach her.

"But you're successful here."

"As a designer and builder, perhaps. Certainly not as a husband or father."

Debra accepted that he'd wanted children and had had none. "Is that why you've never remarried?" He shrugged, and she went on impulsively. "I mean, I feel as though I've failed at something I tried so hard to do right."

"That's a normal feeling, Debra."

"But it's worse in my situation." Without her realizing it, her voice was on the rise. "You heard my conversation with Stuart. My mother has been married three times! Stuart himself regards his marriage as if it were a dog. When he wants it around, he pats its head; when he's not in the mood, he gives it a kick and sticks it in the other room. And look at my work. Characters move in and out of marriage as they would seats in a game of musical chairs—" She caught her breath, then let it out in defeat. "But who am I to criticize anyone? I'm no better. I couldn't make it work, either." Her voice had fallen to a near whisper at the last. What had been a beseechful expression now grew crestfallen.

Graham thought his heart would break. If he'd ever felt inadequate, he did so now. What he wanted to do was to take her in his arms and soothe her, to tell her that it really didn't matter. But it did. At least it did to him. The failure of his marriage had deeply affected his life. And who was *he* to presume to give advice, anyway?

"What did happen to your marriage, Debra?" he heard himself ask softly.

It took her a long while to find the words. When they came, they were barely audible, muted by humiliation. "My husband . . . uh, Jason took to . . . acting out his script with . . . one of his female leads." There. It was out. She wished she felt better for having told him, but she only felt lessened in his eyes.

"He cheated on you."

Her arms tightened around herself. "Yes."

"Just once?"

"Oh-ho, no!" Here the anger revived. "It was the old story of the wife being the last to know. From what I've since learned, it went on for months. The entire cast knew, the whole writing staff knew, everyone else, from executives to technicians, knew. Why didn't *I* know?" she asked in self-derision. *"I* was too busy trusting my husband. I was too sure that *that* would never happen to *my* marriage." She stopped, breathless. "Well, it did," she murmured, suddenly trying to sound philosophical about it but failing miserably. Letting her arms fall from her waist, she dug her hands into the pockets of her jeans. Then she smiled sheepishly at Graham. "Aren't you glad you asked?"

"Yes," he answered without hesitancy. He could understand more now—the cold sound that entered her voice at times, just at times, when she spoke of Jason, the bitterness she directed toward her brother, the firmness with which she declared she'd never return to New York. "But you're wrong, Debra."

She tipped her head. "Wrong? About what?"

"Blaming yourself, for one thing," he said, speaking softly, gently. "If Jason wandered, it was a problem *he* had. I've held you in my arms. There's nothing missing there." Had his voice not been as soothing, his words might have drawn fire. But Debra could only blush.

"There's nothing missing in a medium-rare char-broiled sirloin steak, but even that gets boring after a while."

Graham smiled kindly. "You're not a steak. A steak doesn't write scripts for television. Which brings me to my other point. You're wrong to assume that everyone in the world thinks less of you because your husband cheated. The world can only think less of Jason. And anyone who doesn't isn't worth considering."

Her eyes were misty. "You make it sound so simple. But there's *me*. I feel so disappointed in *myself*. I wanted it to work. I wanted to be different from the others. I wanted to show them it could be done . . ." Her words trailed off, choked by the tightening in her throat. She swallowed hard, then went on in a whisper. "I guess I wanted to *believe* it could be done."

"And now you don't?"

She shook her head.

Very gently, Graham smoothed a strand of hair from her neck. "Maybe you're being too hard on yourself. I mean, your situation is unusual. The work you do, the social circle you've been in—you probably see the worst when it comes to marriage and divorce." His hand remained on her shoulder and seemed to give her a lift.

"You're more optimistic?"

"Regarding myself, not particularly. I've been burned, too. But I've met a lot of wonderful people up here, many of whom have been happily married for years and years. It does have a way of restoring one's faith."

Debra chuckled, amazed that she could do so. "At this point, my faith would need a whole *lot* of restoring."

"It'll come . . . with time." A flicker of doubt momentarily shadowed his eyes, then was gone. "We have to believe that."

Looking up at Graham, she did believe it. There was a strength in him that gave her strength, a gentleness that gentled her. Once again, she realized how refreshing he was, how free of convention in such a wholesome way. And she realized how much better he'd made her feel.

For a minute, standing there, they seemed to share unspoken understandings. Then, sighing deeply, Graham eased his hands down her arms to her hands, where their flesh touched for one warm eon before parting.

"Well." He took a step toward the door. "I've got to be going. I'll, uh, see you Monday morning?"

She smiled and nodded, then watched him pull the

door open and start through. "Graham?" He paused to look back. "Thanks."

Tipping two fingers off his temple, he smiled. "It's all part of the job." Then he continued over the threshold and closed the door behind him.

Debra followed his tall, lithe form as it strode comfortably down the walk. As she watched him ease himself into the pickup, start its motor, then back out of the drive, her mind backed over the hour they'd just shared, and a delightful sense of warmth filled her. There were no thoughts of the man who had forcefully seduced her that morning. He seemed to have departed while she'd been out driving off her anger. On her return, she had found a friend, one who had experienced some of the same agony she had, one who could understand.

Still standing at the window moments later, she studied the empty roadway and was infinitely grateful that she had Monday to look forward to.

It was the start of May and beginning to warm, with a smell in the air that hinted at good things to come. The sun was bright, the breeze fresh. Debra felt better than she had in weeks.

Rising early, she worked quickly to strip her bed and make the first of many trips to the carriage house with her things. Bathed in morning's warmth, the loft was cheery and inviting. As Debra neatly stowed clothes and suitcases under the eaves, she was ever on the lookout for Graham's truck. When it finally appeared on the road and turned in at the drive, she felt more buoyant than ever.

But if she faced the day brightly, Graham was positively gray. She saw it in his face the instant he stepped from the truck, heard it in his voice when he poked his head in at the front door of the main house.

"Debra!"

His holler caught her already en route from the carriage house. "I'm here, Graham," she called, rounding the corner of the house to meet him in front.

He looked tired, as though he'd either spent a sleepless weekend or was one step removed from being hung over. Though clean and well-groomed, looking fresh enough in jeans and a T-shirt with a denim work shirt thrown over it and left open, his eyes spoke of something amiss.

Had they been alone, Debra might have asked if he was all right. But he had a helper, a pleasant-looking young man with dark, mussed hair and a homespun look, who kept his place several steps away. Seeing the two of them—one as muscular and ready to move the earth as the other—reminded her that Graham might well have done his weekend time with the guys at a local pub. In as rural an area as this, that had to be common practice.

She smiled shyly, unsure as to how to greet him. "Uh, hi." She lifted her hand in a quick wave. "I've just been bringing stuff over."

Graham's brows drew together. "We'd have done everything. You should have waited."

Passing her efforts off with a shrug, she forced her eyes from Graham's to those of his friend and extended her hand his way. "I'm Debra Barry."

With a crooked smile, sweet in its bashful way, the dark-haired man gave her hand a firm clasp. "Tom, here." Then he reddened. "Actually, they call me Butch. You might as well, too."

Debra grinned. "Glad to meet you, Butch. And thanks for coming to help. I'm afraid you guys will have your hands full getting that bed up to the loft." Her gaze encompassed Graham, who stared at her solemnly. "I mean, I adore my spiral staircase, but—"

"We've got our ways. I counted on them when I put the staircase in." His voice fell just short of a growl, though that didn't prevent Debra from picturing the lion once more. There was that same studied aloofness she'd seen in him before, the same sense of separation she thought she'd conquered the Friday before.

Feeling discouraged, she forced a smile, if not for Graham then for this man he'd brought along. "Well, then—would either of you like a cup of coffee before you get to it?" She'd long since had the pot ready to go.

Butch's face brightened, and he opened his mouth to accept when Graham headed him off curtly. "Just leave it in the kitchen. I think we'll get started with that bed. Get the worst done first." Motioning for Butch to follow, he stalked into the house, leaving Debra to wonder what she'd done to evoke his wrath.

But she'd done nothing, she decided after several seconds' deliberation. He was simply in a bad mood. Sighing, she returned to the carriage house to continue organizing her things, deeming it better to stay out from underfoot, as Graham so clearly wanted her to do.

She couldn't help but peek, though, following the men's progress as they trudged through the yard with the frame of the large brass bed, brought it carefully through the large double doors and set it down beneath the loft. Taking a seat far off to the side with her legs dangling over the loft's edge, she made her presence as unobtrusive as possible while she watched them fuss with a pile of ropes and pulleys. To her astonishment, it *was* simple, at least to one as mechanically inclined as was Graham. In no time at all, the large bed was hoisted into the air, eased over the railing of the loft and successfully installed beneath the transparent dome.

"Terrific!" she exclaimed, standing back in admiration. "It fits there perfectly!"

Hands on his hips, Graham nodded his agreement,

then bent to collect the discarded paraphernalia. It was Butch who spoke up.

"Does look pretty nice. Good spot. The light's fine." His voice had the sound of the native, a distinct accent that Graham so obviously lacked.

"I think so," Debra remarked, smiling. "The way the sun pours through that dome, it's a natural heater."

Butch cocked a brow. "May get warm in another month."

"That's okay. I like warm. And besides, with those big double doors open, there'll be plenty of breeze."

A gruff sound from below interrupted them. "You're not going to leave the doors open at night, not with *my* equipment in here!" The bark was followed by the appearance of Graham's head just far enough up the stairs to send her a meaningful glance before lowering again.

"Not at night," Debra called after him. "But during the day, I intend to!" Her declaration was as bold as his had been and was accompanied by a wink at Butch. When Graham made no further response, she smiled. "As if someone might want his old equipment," she quipped, keeping her voice low. "What they'll really want is the new lamp I bought last weekend." Her eyes widened. "Do you live nearby, Butch?"

"Yes, ma'am. Just on the other side of town."

"You live with your family?" In Debra's estimation, he had barely passed twenty.

"Yes, ma'am."

"No 'ma'am,' please. That might be my mother. I'm Debra."

He grinned. "Right, Debra. There's my mom and dad and four younger brothers."

"Five boys? And they're all as tall as you?" He had to exceed the six-foot mark.

"Naw. But I'm the oldest. They just haven't got there yet—"

"Butch!" Another growl from below. "A hand!" The head poked up. "If, that is, I'm not disturbing anything." Sharp amber eyes moved pointedly from one to the other of the two in the loft.

Debra and Butch exchanged looks of barely concealed amusement before the latter shrugged and disappeared down the stairs. Feeling guilty at so idly watching the men work, Debra reached for the fresh bedding she'd brought up earlier and set to work.

"Do the cartons in the dining room go up to the loft?" Graham called from below minutes later.

She stopped and thought. "No, why don't you stack them down there. It's only the stuff in the living room that I need here." As she stood quietly, expectantly, she heard his footsteps recede. With a billowing puff, she spread the top sheet over its mate. Only when she'd finished, when the pillows had been fluffed and the pale-blue and cream quilt lay crisply atop it all, did she return to her survey of the men's progress.

Box after box, most of what the moving truck had delivered, found its way to the lower back wall. There seemed, from her viewpoint, a rhythmic pattern whereby Graham would appear with a box, stack it and disappear; then Butch would appear and go through the same routine before yielding his place once more to Graham.

From her perch, Debra watched silently. Each man knew she was there and shot her intermittent glances. Graham's were dark and enigmatic, Butch's lighter and more friendly. It was to the latter that she finally dared speak.

"Do you do this for a living, Butch?" she called down, standing with her elbows propped on the railing and her hands loosely clasped.

"Moving things?" He laughed. "No, ma'am . . . uh, sorry. I go to school."

"You do?" she exclaimed in pleasure. "Where?"

"U.N.H. That's the University of New Hampshire. I'm supposed to be home studying for exams. But when Graham called, I couldn't resist the chance to get out." Having shifted his carton to the top of the pile, he stood with his arms hanging awkwardly by his sides.

"What are you studying?" she asked enthusiastically.

"Veterinary medicine. I love animals."

Debra was fascinated. "You want to be a vet? That's great!"

Graham appeared just then with another armload, effectively ending the conversation with a scowl. Reminded of his job, Butch turned quietly and headed back to the house, leaving Debra to fend for herself. Indulgently patient, she simply watched Graham take his turn and leave, then picked up with the conversation when Butch returned.

"Have you always had animals at home?"

He seemed as ready to talk as she. "At my place? Naw. One of my brothers gets this awful allergic reaction to anything with fur, so I've never been able to have pets of my own. But the neighbors have plenty, and their neighbors and their neighbors." He nodded his head in a gesture of endlessness. "There are plenty of animals in the county. We could use another vet." He heaved the box into place.

"So you'd like to set up shop here?" Funny, the myth was that country kids left for the city as soon as their parents excused them from milking the cow. At least, she thought with amusement, that was the belief held by city folk, who would naturally want to assume that *their* way was everyone else's dream.

"Here . . . or someplace else in the state," Butch returned.

"You like the quiet life?"

He gave a toothy grin. "Quiet life? Hell—excuse me,

ma'am—things really buzz around here sometimes. Take last Saturday at the old textile mill by the river. This fellow from Boston is proposing to turn it into an expensive condominium complex, and the folks around here are fightin' mad—"

Graham was back. Again, the talk died. Butch retreated. Graham eased a carton to the floor to start a new pile. Then, instead of going back for another as Debra had expected, he looked up at her, cocked his hands on his hips and started up the stairs.

As Debra watched him, she felt an apprehension that was only mildly eased by the knowledge of Butch's imminent return. When Graham planted himself not three feet away from her, she straightened and faced him.

"What are you doing with Butch?" he asked, his voice deep and intense.

Debra frowned. "I'm talking to him. He's a nice boy."

"What was that?"

"He's a nice boy." Only when she'd repeated it herself did she realize that Graham had heard her the first time. Only then did her suspicions take root.

"He's a nice *boy*. You remember that." It was the brow he arched and the sharpness of his tongue, even more than his words, that riled her. When he turned to go, she reached out impulsively and grabbed his arm.

"Wait a minute, now. Just what do you mean by that?" She was vaguely aware of Butch's making another trip, then leaving, and was more keenly aware of the flex of Graham's biceps beneath her fingers. Burned, she dropped her hand.

"I mean," Graham began slowly, dangerously, "that Butch is young and impressionable. He'd have no idea how to deal with a woman like you, and I'd hate to think of him having to try. He's got a lot on his mind right now. He doesn't need puppy love."

"He's pleasant and friendly, which is a lot more than I can say for you today."

"He's got a job to do. And so do I. And while we're on that score, I'd better warn you that there'll be other men working here on and off during the next few months. If you're not careful, word will spread—"

"That *I'm* friendly?"

His eyes were cool. "That you're on the prowl. You know, wealthy divorcée hits the backwoods in search of rugged bear type . . ."

"That's disgusting, Graham!" she cried, then lowered her voice when Butch reappeared. "And I'm *not* wealthy!"

"You're divorced and available."

"I am divorced. I am *not* available!"

"Is that why you were out all weekend?"

"What?"

"I tried your line both days. You weren't home. For a woman who's supposedly seeking escape from the hectic city life, you're very active."

"And you assume that I spent the weekend carousing?" Her voice rose again. "Hah! *You're* the one looking half hung over!" She swallowed hard. "It happens that I drove north, up through the mountains. And since I had only myself to please, I decided on the spur of the moment to stop at an inn for the night. It was a very relaxing trip," she mused in recollection, then hardened when she recalled the matter at hand. "As for your sordid imagination, it's gone haywire. I was alone . . . all weekend . . . except, of course, for the innkeepers and their other guests and the waitresses in the restaurants and the fellow who put gas in the car and the lovely old lady at the Kancamagus Highway information booth." She paused only for a breath. "But no, I didn't seduce some yo-yo along the way. I'm not *that* hard up!"

Aware that Butch was due back momentarily, Graham made a conscious effort to keep his voice low. "Is that what last Friday was all about, Debra? You came pretty close to begging."

Her first impulse was to slap him across the face. Her second, as the entire discussion began to fall into place, was to grin, which she did with growing delight. "Why, Graham Reid, I do believe you're jealous."

"Jealous? Me? Of whom?"

"Of Butch . . . or any other man who might cross my path." Her grin stuck, and she crossed her arms saucily over her breasts. "You're jealous."

He glowered. "Jealous? Not on your life! You've got nothing I want."

"No?" she teased, sidling closer, speaking very softly. "I felt you, too, last Friday. Men have that disadvantage, you know."

For a long minute, Graham said nothing. Debra stood barely a breath away looking up at him, convinced that she was right, though praying she hadn't gone too far. She saw him inhale, saw the thin fabric of his T-shirt stretch more tautly across his chest, saw him grow that much taller. Then, very slowly, he smiled.

"You're a crafty one, Debra Barry. Got an answer for everything. I can see why you're good at your trade. Dialogue is your specialty."

Deeply affected by his smile, Debra could do nothing but answer it with a shyer rendition of her own. How he could stir her up one minute, then calm her with a smile, she would never know. But he'd done it.

"Listen, Graham," she began softly. "For what it's worth, I really *don't* have any designs on Butch . . . or any other man. You, of all people, should know how I feel."

Graham eyed her enigmatically. Then, with neither a yea nor a nay, he turned, went downstairs and headed back to the house as Butch burst in with the mail.

"I managed to ambush George." He waved the

handful of envelopes as he walked toward the loft. "This is it for the day." Reaching up, he passed the bundle to Debra, who'd come halfway down the stairs to meet him. "Hope it's good."

Spying the familiar mailer with its even more familiar logo on the left-hand corner, she grinned. "It is. This"—she waved the large manila envelope, clamping the other letters under her arm—"will keep me busy for the week." It was her plot outline, which she proceeded to read perched on a midheight step while Butch rejoined Graham.

When Graham returned from his coffee break, she was on the floor of the carriage house, struggling with a screw that wouldn't turn.

"What are you doing?" he asked in good-humored puzzlement, passing an eye over the long piece of butcher block on which she knelt.

"It's my desk," she grunted, grimacing against the stubbornness of the screwdriver, trying once more, then dropping the useless tool. "This is ridiculous. The man said"—she lightened her voice to one of singsong mockery—"that I'd just have to screw in the legs, and . . . bingo, I'd have my desk." She raised plaintive eyes to Graham. "Why do they always do that . . . make it sound so simple when it isn't?"

Hunkering down, Graham lifted a screw for momentary study. Amusement played at the corner of his mouth. "Because there are those of us who couldn't write a letter home if our lives depended on it. On the other hand, we're great at handling screws. Hold on a second." He returned to the truck and was back moments later with a hand drill that he proceeded to plug into a newly installed outlet. Then he knelt beside the board, made appropriate markings with a pencil and applied the drill to each of the four corners in turn.

"There," he said with satisfaction. "Try it now." Upending one desk leg, he held it in place while Debra attacked the screw once more. Within minutes, the leg was attached.

"That was cheating," she teased.

"It worked, didn't it?" Taking the screwdriver from her, he gave each of the screws a final hard twist, then positioned the next leg.

"There are those of us who would drill the hole, only to have the screw slide in and out."

"The secret," he half-whispered conspiratorially, "is to make the hole at least two or three bit sizes smaller than the screw. The point is simply to give the tip of the screw an entrée, then let its teeth work on their own."

"Very clever." She easily secured the second leg.

"It would be even more clever to use the drill to put the screws themselves in. But that defeats the purpose."

"The purpose?"

"Of doing it yourself." He grew suddenly more earnest. "If things are so simple that there's no expenditure of energy on the task, it'd be just as well to hire someone else to do it. The reward is building up calluses and a sweat, feeling tired at the end of the day."

"Even more than just getting the job done?" she asked, feeling herself on the verge of getting a glimpse of that inner Graham.

He held the third leg in his hand just prior to positioning it and smiled gently. "Yes. Even more than that. I imagine you feel the same way about your job. Those were outlines?"

She hadn't thought he'd noticed her reading. "Uh-huh. Plot summaries for the week's writing."

"How detailed are they?"

"Not very. I get roughly ten pages of outline for every sixty pages of script I'm expected to produce."

"So you have the freedom to put whatever words you want in the mouths of your characters?"

"Pretty much. That's where the challenge comes in. The end result can vary dramatically depending on what I decide to do."

"And if you didn't have that freedom? If the outlines you received specified everything, so that you only had to mechanically flesh out a preconceived story line?"

"It'd be boring . . . and frustrating."

Graham put the leg in place. "My work's the same. There's got to be some challenge somewhere, some demand either on the mind or the body, some sense of pride in making the effort." Then he smiled more playfully, and her heart skipped a beat. "Of course, getting the job done does matter, too. I mean, that's what the client expects."

"Right." Somehow their roles changed, and Debra found herself holding the leg steady while Graham wielded the screwdriver. She watched his hands work, quickly, nimbly, admiring the ease with which he held the tool and made it function so that at times it seemed nothing more than an extension of his own fingers. Quite incongruously, she recalled the warmth of those fingers, the way they'd touched her, tormented her.

Then the desk was finished, and he deftly turned it over and stood it on its legs for the first time. "Not bad," he said. "Here, let's get it upstairs."

To Debra's astonishment, he tipped the entire board once more, lifting it this time and balancing it on his shoulder for the careful trek up the spiral stairs. Seeming to know precisely where she wanted it, he lowered it beneath the skylights and stood back. "Not bad at all. Where's your typewriter?" Looking around, he spotted it resting beneath an eave and lifted it to the table. Then he raised a finger to rub his chin. "I just hope the two electrical outlets we put in will be enough. What have you got? Typewriter, lamp, television—anything else?"

"There's the clock radio, but that's it. Two is plenty." She chuckled. "I'm not going to be here all *that* long, am I?"

Graham sent her a sharp look and shook his head. "Not if I can help it." Then he glanced more broadly around the loft, finally focusing on its stairs. "I hope this was a good idea," he muttered half under his breath.

But Debra caught him. "What do you mean?"

"I mean," he sighed, "that you're pretty isolated out here. What if you wake up in the middle of the night to use the bathroom?"

"Yes . . . ?"

His eyes darkened. "You'll have to traipse all the way back to the house in the dark."

"There's moonlight." She shrugged, careful to conceal her amusement at his concern.

"Only on a clear night. Even then you're apt to trip over God knows what—that is, if you make it down the stairs in one piece. I don't suppose the spiral will be easy in the dark."

"Graham, I'll be fine," she reassured him patiently. "I'll buy a large flashlight. How does that sound?"

"You should have one of those, anyway," he murmured gruffly.

"Then I'll get one." She felt very accommodating. "Anything else?" she asked flippantly, but felt her flippancy wither when Graham's gaze fell to the bed. The shadows playing atop the quilt, the dance of the sun through newly swelling branches, suddenly took on sensual proportions that were in no way diminished in Debra's imagination when he shifted his warm amber eyes to hers.

For a minute, they stared at one another, reliving the fire of a passion barely discovered. Debra felt the tripping of her pulse, the fluttering of her stomach, the insidious weakness of her knees. Without thinking, she moistened her lips against their sudden dryness.

"Debra . . ." Graham warned in a thick growl. Then he cleared his throat. "No. That's all," he clipped before turning and leaving.

His footsteps had long since faded and disappeared before she could move. Even then, it was first her eyes, hitting that bed again, wondering what it might be like to lie with him. It was some time before she managed to galvanize herself in a more practical direction.

May blossomed with every bit of the beauty Debra had hoped to find in the country. The forsythia exploded into fronds of sunshine, the trees budded, then burst into verdant parasols. The grass slowly began its regeneration, showing daily progress from brown to gray to pale green.

As Graham had predicted, the birds returned from the south in fine feather, filling the air with their mating calls, each species, each song, distinctive and glorious. Debra wondered if they sang louder to counter those human sounds that must have been both unexpected and intrusive, for Graham attacked his work with vigor, stripping inner walls to their barest essentials, tearing down others, starting at the tip of the roof to pry away layers of worn outer shingles.

As for herself, she very comfortably fell into a delightful kind of routine whereby she spent her mornings working at the desk beneath the skylights in the loft, then stopped to eat lunch and to watch the show. Her writing went well; she was able to concentrate far better than she'd ever been able to do in New York, though she half-suspected that it was the lure of watching Graham work in the afternoon that kept her disciplined through the morning.

And she did watch him, sometimes on the sly, peering from the loft at his lithe body balanced on the roof, sometimes with no pretense whatsoever as she talked on the phone, which had, of necessity, remained in the main house. That he was handsome, she'd never doubted. Even as the day wore on and his fresh-showered look became more earthy, she found him all the more attractive. It was the small things she noticed —the way his hair grew damp with sweat and clung to his temples, the way he straightened periodically and flexed his right shoulder, the way he blotted his upper lip with the back of his hand. He was the perfect inspiration for those love scenes she had so often to write, or so she excused her daydreams.

The drama of "Love Games" continued day after day. Harris let Debra invest Selena with some of the spirit she'd wanted; when the script arrived in New York, there was only minor editing done. Debra felt satisfied, and the phone calls from Harris tapered to one a week.

Her mother, on the other hand, called several times a week, much as she'd done when Debra had lived in New York. The cost of long-distance calling was insignificant to her, as was the demand she made on Debra's time. What did concern her were the mechanics of choreographing a wedding extravaganza. Each time she called, there was another point to raise, another problem to discuss. Each call ended with the breathy claim that things were truly getting out of hand. Invariably, when Debra suggested that perhaps her mother wasn't sure about the marriage itself, Lucy Shipman would sigh, offer a resigned "Perhaps you're right, dear" and promptly launch into yet another phase of the planning.

Debra could easily humor her mother. Her brother, Stuart, was another matter. Resentful of Debra's flight from the city, he seemed to make a point of playing on the guilt he hoped existed. When there was none, he picked on something else. Unfortunately, Graham was often it.

"What's *he* doing there?" he'd demand at the start of the call.

"I told you. He's working here."

"As a receptionist? Why does he answer the phone?"

"If he's closer to it, he gets it. I've told you that, too, Stuart. I'm living and working in the carriage house, but the phone company couldn't get the phone out there without all sorts of hassles. And it didn't seem worth it, since I'll be moving back here in no time. Graham's doing me a favor by picking up the phone when I'm slow getting over. Otherwise, it'd ring endlessly, I'd rush over only to pick it up just when someone's hung up, and you'd think I was out running around every day." Not a bad idea, she'd mused more than once, to let the phone ring. Stuart's calls irked her.

"Does he work alone?"

"Most of the time. He's had other people helping every so often, but he prefers to do most of it himself."

"Graham Reid?" Her brother would mull the name around before dropping it with a low-muttered "Hmmmph" and going on to discuss Debra's shirking of her responsibility by "hiding," as he put it, in New Hampshire. For the most part, Debra just let him talk. If he wanted to think she was "hiding," it was his right. She disagreed; that was *her* right.

With each passing day, Debra felt more and more comfortable with her decision. Driving into town several times a week, she easily made friends with the locals, whose aloofness fell prey to her ready smile and her openness. In response to their curiosity, she told them that she was a writer. When one day she happened into the doughnut shop to find the patrons watching the soap opera that followed hers, she dared tell them exactly what she wrote. For a week after that, she was aware of the eyes of the townsfolk scrutinizing her every move, until at last, with the realization that she was still the same "pretty young woman who'd come up from New York," she was accepted as one of them. Indeed, they were protective of her, growing closemouthed about her work with the occasional outsider who might be passing through. It was as if she were their own private treasure, their own secret. In turn, Debra made an extra effort to take the time to talk.

It was really no effort, though. Part of what she'd missed in New York, part of what she'd imagined for so long—walking down a street where storekeepers and townsmen called out to her by name with a wave and a smile—was now a reality. She felt whole and individual in a way she'd never felt before. Smiles came easily. In fact, there was only one situation in which she restrained them, and that was when Graham had other workers at the house. Then she was polite and friendly in a quieter way, using prudence as a precaution against his jealousy.

For, over the days, her relationship with Graham developed into a warm one. Gradually, she felt freer simply to stand and talk with him as he worked. When he was alone, she took to making lunches for two, often of the hearty variety that she'd never eat herself but that Graham wolfed down as though he hadn't eaten in days.

"What *do* you eat?" she asked one afternoon as they picnicked in the sunny back yard on a feast of fried chicken and corn.

"Oh, a little of this, a little of that," he responded with a smirk, holding another drumstick out to her, reclaiming it with the first shake of her head.

"Do *you* cook?"

"Sure."

"I'll bet. I know your type," she teased, eying him askance. "You've got people falling all over you, begging to cook you a meal."

"You didn't seem to fall over me begging." He arched a brow in mischief, to which Debra responded with her most nonchalant shrug.

"I was making lunch, anyway. You just happen to be here to join me."

"You've made plenty." Still he goaded. "You'd really have eaten it all without me?"

"Over several days," she said smartly, then attempted to justify further the size of the meal she'd made. "The best time to eat a big meal is at lunch. Then you can spend the rest of the day burning it off."

Graham very deliberately looked her over, lingering at her breasts, her waist, her hips, sending tingling ribbons throughout her body. "Why am *I* the one doing all the eating?"

"Because *I* don't do much to burn it off."

"Yeah, but if I eat big at lunch, then again at dinner, isn't that pushing it?" He sat straighter, stretched, patted the flat span of his stomach.

"You could always . . . lift weights," she suggested, grinning.

"Are you kidding?" He feigned offense. "I'll have you know that this body used to be skinny. It is what it is today through legitimate work." He arched a brow. "Weight lifting is for those who can't get their muscle tone elsewhere. How about you?" Leaning forward before Debra could anticipate his move, he gently squeezed her arms and legs, then poked at her stomach.

She burst into a peal of laughter that was only partly a result of the tickling. "Stop it, Graham!" she gasped, grabbing his hand to stop the torture. Then he paused. They looked at one another, suddenly more serious, frighteningly close. His hand was warm, warm and large and barely encompassed by her fingers. His eyes fell to her mouth, taking her breath away with no more than a visual caress. Then the cry of a wild goose overhead jolted them, and the spell was broken.

It seemed a pattern. The time they spent together

was filled with lighthearted banter that inevitably ended in a glance, a touch, or a sigh that reminded them of the spark that never quite died. Debra never forced the issue. She was no more ready to take a step toward involvement with Graham than he was with her.

Yet there was a nagging within her, subtle, quiet, most noticeable at night when she was alone in the loft with the moon and stars overhead and the whisper of a breeze in the trees. She chose to interpret it as a growing pain; for the first time, she was a viable, separate entity, neither daughter nor wife, but herself. In her heart, however, she suspected differently. Graham Reid was fast becoming habit forming.

Though she kept busy on weekends exploring the countryside, hiking along quiet streams, shopping at fabled sweater mills, stopping in to visit with new-found friends, Monday mornings were always special. When Graham arrived, her heart beat a little faster, her step was a little lighter, and she felt that little bit richer than she had before. If she didn't know better, she'd suspect herself half in love with the man. But she knew better. She'd just been through an ugly time, coming off a relationship that had, for so long, been her be-all and end-all. Graham was someone she . . . liked, admired, felt a phenomenal physical attraction for. But love? It couldn't be.

Still, she found herself planning those special lunches, making a point to talk with him, to be as open as possible about her work and the phone calls she received. It wasn't a conscious effort to involve him in her life; rather, she found comfort in discussing things with him, found that he could take a situation and help her work it out.

Much as she tried to turn the tables, though, Graham kept the door to his private life locked. He spoke of the present only, or perhaps the immediate local past. As for his upbringing, his education, his marriage, he remained ever evasive.

Debra came to recognize the change in his mood from the sound of his hammer against the new cedar shingles he applied to the roof. There were times when he pounded with ease and confidence, others when the nails clearly bore the brunt of his frustration. At times, when she felt helpless to reach him, her frustration was nearly as great. He seemed troubled then, and she ached to help.

But he refused to let her, forcing her to be content with the gentle, playful, often thoughtful times they shared. Graham was her secret; what they shared, the warmth and closeness, existed only in the small world of her house.

Until the day Jason Barry appeared.

Chapter Seven

June had just begun, and with it, Debra's seventh week in the house. As the weather became truly warm, she spent much of her time outdoors, writing perched in the old wooden swing, walking through the yard and the woods beyond, often simply basking in the sun with an eye on Graham, who, having finished shingling the roof, had moved on to the side walls, working with painstaking care to complete the outer surface of the house before moving inside.

This particular Monday was a quiet one at the house, made all the more peaceful by the stillness of the air, the blueness of the sky, the brilliance of the sun. Barefoot, Debra wore a bandeau top and shorts. Graham was bare-chested and wore faded jeans and sneakers.

It was midafternoon. Debra had done her writing for the day, had barbecued steak sandwiches on the grill for lunch and had diligently taken notes through an hour of "Love Games." She now sat relaxing on the front lawn, her legs stretched before her, her arms propped behind her head, her eyes glued to the bronzed torso of her carpenter.

Her carpenter. It had been a long time since she'd thought of him that way. Yet there he was, high atop a ladder, pounding nails into shingles, looking extraordinarily masculine and unfairly appealing. She recalled the first time he'd shucked his shirt because of the heat. She'd felt shy, skittish, almost afraid to look at him. Even now, though she'd overcome that initial timidity, she still felt the same quickening of her pulse, the same reflexive tightening in the pit of her stomach.

It wasn't that she'd never seen a man before; obviously, she had. But Graham's body was different, more firm and muscular. Glistening with sweat, his skin slid over sinewed cords as he lifted each shingle, positioned it, reached for a nail, exerted the force to drive it home. His arms were long and strong and grew browner by the day. She noticed the way the sun sparkled on their tawny flecks of hair, then, when he turned to reach for another shingle, traced the mat of hair on his chest in its tapering path to his belt.

Lying abruptly flat, she shut her eyes, but the image of his body remained, seeming intensified by her imagination and a heightened awareness of her own gentle curves. When the sound of the phone carried through the open window, she was almost relieved at the diversion.

Graham paused in his work to watch her trot toward the house, thinking how healthy she looked with a tan, how much of the country girl she seemed to have become. It was getting harder to keep his distance, he mused, then turned and poured double-strength energy into pounding another nail.

"Graham?" She leaned out the front screen door. "It's for you. It's Joe." Joe was the fellow who'd been out the week before taking measurements for the new kitchen.

Backing down the ladder, Graham strode to the door, passing her in his silent trek to the phone. While he talked, Debra wandered to the kitchen, imagining the stove and the microwave, the double-door refrigerator, the central island with its open grill that she'd ordered. She returned to the living room in time to see Graham hang up the phone.

"Any problem?" she asked, catching his frown.

"Hmmm? Oh, no. It was nothing. He remembered something he wanted me to pass on to the electrician."

Debra nodded, then sighed in satisfaction and looked around. "It looks so different already, so much larger and brighter."

"It is." He shot a glance through the ceiling that was no more, to the exposed rafters of the second story. "Those windows up there may be small, but they give that much more light than the living room had before. Wait until the skylights go in. Then you'll really see a difference."

She tipped her head back, trying to picture the way it would look. In so doing, she missed Graham's eyes on her, then their shift to the window.

"Someone's here," he said quietly. "Were you expecting anyone?"

Debra whirled around to see a strange car approaching. "Not me." She shrugged, then looked more closely. The car had New Hampshire plates, but its driver had come a bit farther. His thick silver hair and the confident tilt of his head identified him instantly.

"Oh, no!" she whispered in dismay, then raised distressed eyes to Graham. "Oh, no!"

"Who is it?" he asked cautiously, but knew the answer before she gave it.

"It's Jason!" With her lower lip crushed beneath her teeth, she stared at Graham, then whispered a disbelieving "He's not supposed to be here. This is *my* house."

Graham's eyes spoke of understanding, but he said nothing; he simply lifted a gentle hand to her cheek and ran his thumb across it lightly. In that instant, Debra composed herself. When he dropped his arm, she slowly turned and went outside.

Climbing from the car, Jason automatically straightened his linen trousers and fingered his leather belt. His eyes made a wary study of the house before coming to rest on Debra. "Hi, sweetie!" he exclaimed, then looked again at the house. "This is some place you've got."

"What are you doing here, Jason?" she asked, keeping her voice under taut control. Having crossed the yard halfway, enough to discourage his entrance into the house without a specific invitation, she stopped.

Undaunted by the chill of her welcome, Jason made a ceremony of breathing in the fresh air as he patted his lean stomach and took the few steps to meet her. "Visiting you, Deb. I decided it was time I saw the country, after all." He studied her, then took her shoulders and leaned forward. When she flinched and turned her head away, his kiss landed on her cheek. She stepped back as quickly as she could.

"What do you want?" she asked.

"To see how you're doing." He smiled. "You look well. Beautiful, in fact. Tanned, no makeup. Barefoot." When his gaze suddenly shifted, Debra cast a glance behind to see Graham emerge from the house. With a nod in their direction, he returned to his work.

"Is that the Reid fellow Stuart's all huffed about?"

"Yes."

"Doesn't look like anything more than a workman to me." The sharpness of Jason's scrutiny belied the casualness of his tone.

"That's what he is."

"Are you pleased with him?"

"Uh-huh."

"Can I—do you mind if I take a look?"

"From here, no. Go ahead. Then you can get back in your car and return to New York."

"Come on, Deb. What kind of a way is that to talk? I came up here to see you."

She felt stronger by the minute, particularly knowing that Graham was near. "You should have phoned with your plans, and I would have saved you the trip. There's no place for you here, Jason."

He held out a hand to calm her down. "Look, I know you were hurt—"

"Hurt?" Her eyes flashed in anger. She couldn't believe that he'd presumed to come to her house. *Her* house! *"Hurt?"*

"Listen, I can explain."

"It's too late for explanations, Jason. We're divorced. It's over."

"You're being childish—"

"If I displease you, then leave. There's no reason for you to stay."

"Debra, I came here to talk," he began more loudly. Looking up, he caught Graham's stare. "Let's go somewhere." Reaching out, he slipped his fingers around her arm.

Debra pulled free with a sharp tug. "Anything you have to say can be said right here."

Jason lowered his voice until his lips barely moved. "We've got an audience. I'd like some privacy."

"Then go back to New York. You've got the apartment. Go in and close the door. You'll have all the privacy you want." The effort of self-control had begun to take its toll. Debra felt her insides beginning to churn.

"Why are you doing this, Debra? We had something good going."

"We did, didn't we," she observed. "Then *you* destroyed it."

"I'm sorry for that, sweetie. I'll make it up to you."

Debra stared at him in disbelief, gritted her teeth, looked away, then back. "Make it up to me? Are you out of your mind? I don't want *anything* from you . . . except your absence from my life!"

"Shhh. Keep your voice down." He cast an eye toward the house. "Your man there's apt to wonder."

"Graham won't wonder about anything," she bit back in annoyance. "He already knows about us. And if he can't hear what we're saying, I'll probably summarize it for him later."

For the first time, Jason seemed disturbed. Frowning, he fingered the fine-trimmed edge of his sideburn in a gesture Debra used to find endearing. Now it left her cold.

"What's going on, Debra?" His eyes bored into her. "Don't tell me you've taken up with the first man on the scene?"

"And if I have? It's *my* affair, not yours."

"I'm your husband—"

"You *were* my husband." She stood a little straighter. "I'm a free woman now. I can do whatever I want. Besides, who are *you* to pass judgment on me? You were carrying on with another woman while your own wife sat home believing you to be faithful. Don't talk about being my husband," she sneered, then tossed her hair from her cheeks. "You cheated, and now you pay the price."

"So this is punishment—the divorce, your place up here? Is that it?" His tone was low. "You stick the knife in just far enough, then twist it. Not enough to kill, just to hurt . . ."

Debra scowled in disgust. "Ever dramatic, aren't you? Well, save it for your script, Jason. It's wasted on me." Turning on her heel, she started toward the house, only to be spun back when he grabbed her arm.

"Just a minute, now." There was an element of danger, a new tone in his voice, something she'd never heard there before. "I didn't traipse all the way up here only to have you turn your back on me. I don't know what's gotten into you, Debra. You never used to be rude."

Breathing hard, she struggled to keep her temper. "You're right, Jason. I used to be sweet and under- standing. A patsy, in fact." She lowered her eyes to her arm and gave each word its separate weight. "Get your hand off me." Stunned by her tone, Jason released her. Only then did she continue, looking him straight in the eye, taking advantage of his momentary disadvantage. "You know, I really disgust myself. When I think back to all those times I covered for you, writing your portion of the script, believing that you were on the set studying the art of direction . . ." She shook her head. "I was really dumb."

"No, you weren't. You loved me. That's what love is all about. Trust." He paused, ignoring the sudden flare of her nostrils. "Do you mean to tell me that everything you felt is gone?" He snapped his fingers. "Just like that?"

It took every bit of self-restraint for Debra to keep from spitting. "'Just like that'?" she echoed softly. "No, Jason, it didn't go"—she aped his finger snap— "just like that. It was more like this." She drove one fist into the other palm, creating a thud that made both hands sting. She was too upset to notice. "But you're ight. It *is* a matter of trust. When I discovered you'd been playing around, the trust I'd lived by was shat- tered. Demolished." She took a breath. "And it's a funny thing about trust. Once it's gone, it's gone." Her knees were shaking, but her voice softened in sadness. "So, in answer to your question, no, not everything I felt is gone. I remember the good times we had, and there is warmth in those memories. But I can never trust you again, or, for that matter, respect you. Without those two things, love is, well, a farce."

For a long time, Jason said nothing. When he finally

spoke, his voice was hard, signaling his refusal to accept defeat. "You're a dramatist yourself, Debra. No wonder you're such a good scriptwriter."

"Don't flatter me, Jason. It doesn't mean anything anymore. I'm good because you taught me, and I know I'm good because Harris tells me so."

"The show needs you. I'd hate to see you have to bow out."

Debra's breath caught in her throat, held there in part by the malevolent expression on Jason's face, in part by his obvious implication. "Is that a threat?" she whispered at last.

He shrugged. "Not really. It's a reminder that I was instrumental in getting you your position."

"I earned that," she argued vehemently. "I was the one doing all your work!"

"But without me, you'd never have gotten the job."

"And . . . ?" Her blood pounded.

"I swing considerable weight with Harris."

"And . . . ?" She waited for the other shoe to fall.

He took a deep breath. "Well . . . I know that Janice Walker is just dying for your job."

Debra stood with her mouth open, her entire being stunned by disbelief. It wasn't that she felt threatened, not for a minute. Harris knew of her talent and would just as easily can Jason as her. But the utter gall of Jason to even suggest it . . .

"What is it you want, Jason?" she seethed. "Why did you come here? The bottom line, now. All evasion aside."

He looked levelly at her. "I want you back, Debra. I want you to come back to New York with me as my wife."

With great effort, she restrained a laugh. "Go on. How would you explain this sudden reconciliation to everyone?"

He had it all worked out. "It would be simple enough to say that we patched things up. That we can't live without each other. That we're in love."

"But we're not. And we won't be."

"I want you by my side."

"Why?"

He seemed to flounder, as though unprepared for such a prodding demand. "Because . . . that's where you belong."

Fists balled, Debra widened her eyes. The anger that had begun to heat suddenly neared the boiling point. Her voice was low, trembling with fury. "That has to be the phoniest line you've thrown me yet!" she cried. "And I don't buy it, any more than I buy the idea that you can get me fired."

Whirling, she took a step, then turned back. "You know what I think? I think you're in the midst of one hell of a midlife crisis. That's what your thing with Jackie was about. That's what your need for me is about. It's the image, isn't it, Jason?" Her voice rose an octave. "You want me back because you can't bear the idea of your wife dumping you. You thought you could have it all—me, Jackie, any other little leading lady who came along. I can almost imagine you telling everyone how understanding I'd be." Her eyes flooded, and she gasped in dismay. "Well, I'm not! I have my pride *and* my self-respect. The *last* thing I'd do is go back with you!" She held out a shaking finger. "So you can get into that little rental car of yours and take yourself back to New York. I don't want you, Jason! It's as simple as that!"

He took her arm again. "Listen, sweetie—"

"Don't 'sweetie' her," a deep, slow, steel-edged voice interrupted, "and get your hand off her arm." Both heads turned as Graham came to stand by Debra's side. Debra had never seen his amber eyes as livid. "The woman has told you to leave several times now." He cocked his head toward the drive. "I'd suggest you get going."

Jason was taken aback for only a minute before he drew himself straighter. A six-footer himself, he lacked only two or three inches on Graham. The difference was glaring, in build even more than in height.

"Who do you think *you* are? This is a private matter between my wife and myself," Jason stated indignantly.

With slow deliberation, Graham slid an arm around Debra's waist and drew her gently to his side. She felt his comfort instantly and leaned against his strength. "She's not your wife. Try again."

He did, but on a different tack. "What is this, Debra? Since when do you need a bodyguard? Are you *that* afraid of me or simply afraid of yourself? Would it be that horrible to admit you still love me?"

Graham remained silent, sensing Debra's need to answer on her own. The faintest flex of his fingers on her shoulder restored her self-command, enabling her to answer in a surprisingly steady voice. "Graham isn't my bodyguard. He's my friend . . . which is more than you were during those last months. And no, I'm not afraid of you *or* myself. You killed whatever love I may have once felt. It's just not there anymore." Her voice lowered to an urgent whisper, made so by the emotional strain of a remembered betrayal. "Leave, Jason! Leave me alone! This house, this land, is fresh and new for me. I don't want a single memory of you here."

Her knees threatened to buckle, but she gritted her teeth and willed herself to stand. What did the trick was Graham's support, that simple hand on her left shoulder, that pillar of warmth by her right side.

Jason glowered. "I'm disappointed in you, Debra" was all he said before throwing a venomous glance at Graham, turning and stalking haughtily toward his car.

Debra didn't move. She stood watching, waiting until

Jason's angry foot on the accelerator backed the car from the drive, whipped it down the road and out of sight. Then, in the aftermath of his visit, she began to tremble. Slowly and smoothly, Graham turned her into his arms and drew her close, pressing her cheek to the warm flesh of his chest, her ear to his heart. His arms closed about her back, simply holding her tight. Barefooted, she seemed smaller, more vulnerable. He bent his head until his cheek lay against the chestnut silk of her hair and closed his eyes, concentrating on absorbing her anguish as best he could.

With a soft moan, she wrapped her arms around his waist and held to him convulsively. Her breath came in ragged gasps that she tried to steady by inhaling deeply. It worked. The natural scent of his flesh was a relaxant, the strength of his arms a sedative, the steel of his thighs a buttress for the insidious weakness of her knees. Again and again, she breathed in, sometimes with a quiet moan, other times with nothing more than a wispy sigh. It was as though she wept tearlessly, fighting off the image of Jason as she clung to Graham.

And he held her steadily, his hands tentatively rubbing her back, coaxing wire-taut muscles to relax. It was all he could do not to speak, to tell her how proud he was of her, to assure her she'd done the right thing. But then she could accuse him of gloating, and he didn't want that. The good will that had built between them was precious to him, nearly as much as was the trust. He wanted neither threatened.

Debra felt the quickening of his heart and instinctively rubbed her cheek against him. The contrast she found was delightful, warm flesh with its soft mat of hair, stretched firm over his powerful chest. She felt safe and comfortable, as though she'd found the spot where she could easily spend the rest of her life. Jason wasn't here; he could never be. There was only Graham and the richness of the earth.

Eyes closed, she breathed deeply again, this time reveling in the maleness of his scent, so lusty and pure. It seemed somehow to have pushed her beyond sedation to the brink of intoxication, and she had neither the strength nor the desire to resist its pull. Turning inward, she put her lips to his chest and kissed it lightly once, then again. Then she slipped her hands from his waist, up his back, to explore that span of flesh and sinew. Her pulse raced on its own this time, keeping pace with that other beat by her ear.

"Debra?" Graham's hoarse voice held a question.

Tightening her arms once more, she slowly looked up at him. Her eyes took in the warmth of his, the faint flush on his cheeks, the readiness of his lips. This wasn't Jason; there was no similarity whatsoever. This face held a wealth of caring, of understanding, of selflessness. This was Graham, and she wanted desperately to kiss him.

Standing on tiptoe, she touched her lips to his chin, kissing it lightly, then dropping similarly gentle kisses around the chiseled corner of his mouth. Drawing back once, she met his gaze. Its heat was confirmation of the story told by his constricting muscles and the more rapid rise and fall of his chest.

When she stretched up again, his arms tightened to lift her, and his lips parted to welcome her. Their kiss was one of a mutual hunger suddenly unleashed after days of restraint. It was a devouring, a total consummation, a ravaging that left Debra breathless and light-headed.

Her arms slipped forward, her hands feeling the surprising softness of the skin at his side before inching up his chest, between their bodies, and creeping over the brawny slope of his shoulders. Her body was stretched up against him, held in place now by her arms encircling his neck, freeing his hands to explore her back. All the while their lips clung to one another's, as though afraid of what even the briefest separation might bring.

It had to come, though, as their lungs craved the air demanded by fast-burgeoning arousal. With a throaty groan, Graham tore his mouth away and buried it against her neck. "Debra," he whispered, then set his tongue to tracing circles just below her ear.

Debra thought she'd explode under the fiery, moist assault. Arching her neck to give him even greater access, she was unaware of the fierceness of her grip on his neck, mindless of the soft sounds of satisfaction that escaped her throat. When he sank to the ground, she flowed with him, never once releasing him.

He held her across his lap, one hand behind her shoulders in support, the other free to touch her. As they sat there on the lawn looking at one another, the rest of the world receded. Debra knew only that she felt whole and loved, that Graham had driven all thought of pain and betrayal from her mind. A gentle smile softened her lips when his fingers warmed her cheek. When his thumb reached to draw the outline of her mouth, she caught it and kissed it. She let go of his neck then, but only to bring one hand down to capture his fully, to press his palm to her lips, to sample the roughness of the calluses that so symbolized his work. As she stared at him over the tips of his fingers, she knew she wanted more, much more.

Pressing his fingers against her cheek, she tried to speak. "Graham . . . I . . ." But the words wouldn't come. What could she say? That she loved him? It could well be true, though she wasn't ready to hear it herself. That she wanted him? But he knew that already, and she couldn't beg for him as she'd once done. What, then, was there? "Graham . . ."

He freed the tip of one of those fingers to seal her lips. "Don't say a word, love," he murmured. "Nothing

matters but this"—he kissed one eye, then the other—
"and this. I only want to make it better."

"It is," she whispered, her lips softly parted. When
he cupped her chin and lowered his head, she was
waiting, eager to please him in turn. She gave him
everything, her lips, her tongue, the heady blend of
sweetness and fire in each. And in the giving, she was
the recipient of an even greater excitement, for as she
stimulated him, he grew bolder. His hand slipped to her
neck, fitting gently to it before sliding lower. Her throat
was bare, as was her chest above the top of the
elasticized bandeau. She felt his fingers against her
flesh, knew the textured gentleness of his workman's
hands. When they skimmed the bandeau, she felt her
body swell instinctively upward.

"Graham . . ." His name was an extension of her
thoughts.

His lips fanned her forehead as he whispered, "Let
me touch you."

"Yes . . . oh, yes . . ." Eyes closed, she arched her
back, then gasped when she felt his hand slip down to
her breast. With knowing fingers, he caressed her
fullness, seeming to measure it against the constricting
fabric. Easily finding its nubbed tip, he pushed his
thumb up and back. Debra squirmed at the charge of
white-hot flashes his manipulation sent to her core.
Unknowingly, she raked her fingers through the hair on
his chest and clung.

"Oh, Graham . . ."

"Feel good?" Their voices matched in soft-whispered
intimacy.

"Mmmmmm. Does it ever."

"Want more?"

She opened her eyes to find nothing but sincerity in
his eyes. "Yes," she murmured without hesitancy. Her
body was afire with the heat of his touch; the coiled

tension within her would not have permitted any other answer.

"Kiss me," he rasped, and she did with passion. Through a haze of delight, she was abundantly aware of his fingers easing the bandeau down over her breasts.

Laying her gently back on the ground, Graham used both hands to shimmy the top to her waist. Then, with the muscles of his shoulders bunched as he propped himself on his hands, he gazed down. Debra lay still, aware of her breasts and their tautened peaks, savoring the pleasure Graham seemed to find in her ripeness. Though never an exhibitionist, as had been some of the women she'd known in her time, she felt no shyness now. What she offered Graham was nothing more than what had seemed his all along.

"You're lovely, Debra." His rasping voice and worshipful gaze made her believe it. Lifting his hand, he touched her skin, gently at first but with tingling effect. "So soft and pale," he murmured in fascination. "Not tanned here. If the sun only knew what it missed . . ." He ran his fingers around one breast before palming its nipple with the same seductive rotation. It was sweet torture for Debra, who moaned and reached for his wrist. "I'm hurting you?" he asked, instantly cautious.

"Oh, yes," she breathed with a timid smile, "but not there."

Leaning forward, Graham touched his lips to hers. "Then where?" he whispered against the corner of her mouth. "Here?" He blindly reached for the other breast and found it with unerring accuracy. When she gasped and shook her head, he lowered his hand to span her midriff. "Here?" Again, she shook her head, this time nipping at the tongue she found tasting her lower lip. Then he leaned lower until the swells of his chest brushed her nipples, and he extended his arm over her hip and down her leg before drawing his fingers back against her thigh. "Here?"

Her thigh quivered. "No. . . . Oh, Lord, Graham
. . . you can't imagine—" Her voice died in her throat
when his hand stole upward to caress gently her
warmest throbbing. She arched instinctively, seeking
relief from the knot he'd tied her in, then let out an
anguished moan when his fingers only worsened the
torment with their play. "Graham—" This time, his lips
cut her off, opening hers even wider in a kiss as explicit
as any she'd ever experienced. It was a mating of
tongues, a combustive welding of everything moist and
hot.

She knew what she wanted then, knew it as she
should have that very first day she'd met Graham.
"Graham . . ." she whispered into his mouth. When he
raised his head, she brought her hands up to frame his
face. "What do you want?" she asked, her eyes brimming with the need to give.

He slid his hand up her body, over her stomach and
breasts to her wrist. With gentle insistence, he brought
her hand down again, pressing it at last against the
proof of his desire. "I want you, love," he rasped,
holding her hand against him, coaxing it back and
forth. His breathing grew more labored by the minute.
"I want all of you—every inch of your flesh against
mine. I want you naked in my arms and eager in my
bed. God, Debra," he cried in a voice deep and as
anguished as her whispers had been, "I don't think I
can stand much more of this." He yanked her hand up
and pinned it to the ground by her shoulder. "I want to
be in you, damn it, not imagining what you had with
Jason or what you're thinking and feeling when you
write your love scenes!"

The force of his words took them both by surprise, as
did the words themselves. They were an intrusion on
the uniqueness of the moment, a stark reminder of that
other world from which Debra had come, of which she
was in many respects still a part. And Graham was the

carpenter once more, the eminently physical man. But he'd been that all along, she argued silently, then caught herself.

No, he hadn't! During these moments of lovemaking, he'd been as tender and thoughtful as the most cultured of gentlemen. There had been nothing coarse about him, nothing to demand his own gratification above hers. Who was he, she asked herself as she lay half-naked beneath him? She barely knew, despite the intimacy they'd shared.

"What is it, Debra?" Graham asked, his vehemence held in sudden check when he sensed the change in her mood.

Her voice was little more than a whisper, her eyes an amalgam of yearning and fear. "I hardly know you. I can't believe it."

"You know what there is to know—what's important."

"And what's that?" she asked unevenly.

"That I'm a man, living alone here in the country, earning an honest living for himself."

"But that's now, Graham." She spoke more firmly as her thoughts began to gel. "What about the past?"

He tightened the muscle in his jaw for a minute, then released her hands and rolled from her to sit by her side, staring out at the countryside while she awkwardly pulled the bandeau back in place.

"It doesn't matter," he gritted, warm passion now a memory.

"It does. That's just it," she argued softly, sitting up to face him. The moment of sensuality had been lost, sacrificed to something she felt to be more important. "What we are in life is the sum of all those little parts." Her gaze sought the horizon. "I'm here today because of everything I was and did and saw before." She turned back to look at his stern profile. "You can understand me because you know where I've been.

Even your seeing Jason today must have been enlightening."

He eyed her sharply. "It was. He has to be nearly twenty years older than you are."

She shrugged. "Not quite, but close enough. And what you're thinking is right. I suppose there was a bit of the father figure in him that appealed to me when I met him. He took me under his wing as his protégée. I never thought to question what he did."

"I can understand that," he said more gently.

"Then you can also understand why being here, doing my thing, standing on my own two feet, has to mean a lot to me."

"I do."

"See?" Her eyes brightened. "You *can* understand. As for me"—she paused, then frowned—"I find you a big question mark. You leave here at the end of the day and go to a place I can't picture. You take off on Fridays and do . . . *whatever* . . . all weekend. When Monday morning comes, I don't dare ask for fear you'll clam up and get angry. I know you were married, but I don't dare ask about your wife or where you lived or where you lived before that or where you learned to design the way you do . . ." Running out of breath, she came to an abrupt halt. Then she looked at him gently, beseechingly. "*Can* I ask you those things, Graham? Would you answer me?"

For a while, he said nothing. His eyes skipped from hers to the ground, to the distant hills. He knew he was being unfair; he had told himself so before. He'd been well aware that in their discussions Debra was always the one to open up. Now, as he looked at her, he realized all that he wanted to tell her. Yet there was still one part that held back, one part that feared himself lost if he confided in her. His last bastion would be breached; he would be totally vulnerable.

Did it really matter, he asked himself, as he studied her face again? Was he heart-whole, even now? He hadn't wanted this job, but he'd taken it. He hadn't wanted her friendship, but it had happened with the inevitability of the sunrise. He hadn't wanted her passion—only her body. Even there, things hadn't worked as he'd planned. And now—could he escape what was probably already fact? Was he in love with her?

Pushing himself to his feet, he dropped his gaze to hers, purposely playing on the advantage of his height to compensate for the helplessness he felt. But the knitting of his brows betrayed his troubled thoughts. "I'm not ready, Debra. . . . I'm sorry." Clearing his throat, he turned, mumbled a quiet "I'd better get back to work" and left.

Dismayed, Debra followed his determined stride as it took him across the lawn and back to the house, his ladder, hammer, nails and shingles. It stunned her to think how much had passed since he'd last left his perch. She ran an absent hand along the smooth skin of her upper arm, then squeezed it tight as the pounding nearby resumed with a vengeance.

It hadn't been *that* bad, she reasoned with herself. Though she hadn't learned anything, at least he hadn't slammed the door in her face. She could afford to be patient for a while. Neither of them were going far. If only there weren't this nagging ache of unfulfillment.

Swiveling around so that her back was to Graham, she hugged her knees to her chest. It was small solace that he, too, seemed to have a surplus of nervous energy, if the ferocity of his hammering was indicative of his state. Fortunately for him, he had that outlet. As for her . . .

With the popping of the solution into mind, she was on her feet and headed for the carriage house, her purse and keys. She didn't spare a glance at the house when she backed from the drive.

On her return, she looked only long enough to see that Graham had made spectacular progress in her absence. But then, she'd expected as much, what with the fervor of his attack.

Pulling the Blazer in on the far side of his truck, she climbed out and opened the back. Then she reached in and gave a tug at the machine that her friend in the hardware store had stowed there so easily. It wouldn't budge.

"Damn!" Gritting her teeth, she applied both hands and managed to inch the offending object closer. On impulse, she climbed in and used the full force of her body to maneuver it to the door. Scrambling out once more, she managed to wrestle it to the very edge of the car so that she could lower it to the ground. Then, breathless and frustrated, she stood back for a minute to eye the steel contraption. It was only when she reached to encompass it once more that Graham's voice froze her.

"My God, Debra!" he exclaimed, closing in fast to push her aside and haul the resister to the ground. "What are you trying to do? Wrench every muscle in your body?"

"*You* just lifted that thing," she replied with indignation as she mopped dampness from her forehead with the back of her hand. "So did Pat at the hardware store. Neither of you had any trouble with it."

"But you're a woman," came the growling retort. "You can't do that."

"Says who?" Her eyes were bright; she was ready for a fight.

"Says me," he announced, but his eyes were suddenly gentle and his voice soft enough to take the wind from her sails. "You can't weigh much more than a hundred pounds."

"You're ten short. Playing it safe?"

He grinned. "You bet. But the point is that *I* have a lot more bulk. Come to think of it, Pat's even bigger. We've got more of an edge on this thing"—he eyed the machine—"than you do, not to mention the fact that our lives are physically oriented. Yours isn't. And"—he emphasized the words with a quirk of his brow—"if you're going to accuse me of being chauvinistic, save your breath. If you were five-ten and weighed in at one-seventy, I'd let you carry your own damned roto-tiller. Now"—he took a breath—"what had you planned to do with it, anyway?"

"Put in a garden," she answered simply, robbed of a suitable barb by his irrefutable logic.

"Where? In back?"

"Uh-huh. The sun's best there."

"Flowers?"

She shook her head, then pried a strand of damp hair from her cheek. "Vegetables."

"Ahhhhh. A victory garden."

"Of sorts." She cocked her head to the side. "I've never grown my own food before. It'll be a challenge."

Graham cast her a skeptical look. "You know what to do?"

"Sure. I spent time at the library in Manchester last weekend. I've got several books here. But I have to turn the soil before I do anything else. Hence"—she scowled at the machine—"*this*." Then she took a breath and reached for its handle, intending to wheel it to the back yard. "I might as well get to it. It's getting late."

Graham was kind enough not to comment on the hour. Both knew that it was a chore best begun in the morning; both knew, though, that even the short time she'd have now would be therapeutic. Only Graham knew, however, that the task was easier said than done.

"Here," he offered magnanimously, "let me bring it out back for you. It's not the easiest thing to push."

Debra watched, thinking that it didn't look all that hard. When he'd positioned it where she wanted it and she took the helm, however, she was in for a rude awakening. It moved. That was something. But slowly. And with great effort. She'd barely made it halfway down the first lap, and she'd already broken into a sweat again.

"Want me to get it going?" Graham asked. He stood to the side with his hands on his hips, looking annoyingly complacent.

Hearing the subtle humor in his voice, she grew all the more adamant. "No, thanks." She ended on a high note. "I'll do it." And she pushed the tiller a little farther, then a little farther still, until she ran into something hard and couldn't proceed. Kicking at the soil, she uncovered the problem. *"Rocks?"* She hadn't planned on them and silently cursed the books she'd read for the omission.

"You bet. Most of New England is rocky. It's not quite as bad here as it is farther south and toward the coast, though."

"Hmmph, that's encouraging. But how do I get it out?"

"You dig it up either with a pick or a shovel. Got either?" She shook her head, a look of dismay on her face. "Then run and get the shovel from the truck. It should be in back." When she returned moments later, Graham had already made his third turn with the tiller. "You get that rock," he directed without stopping. "It's not too big."

It wasn't. After dislodging it without too much fuss, she managed to heave it to the side, then stood back to watch Graham work. *To watch Graham work.* For nearly an hour, that was what she did. Oh, there were occasional rocks to be removed, but even then he took care of most with his bare hands. All she could do was to watch the work of his muscles as they rippled beneath the bronzed skin of his shoulders, chest and arms. As he built up a sweat, the late-afternoon sun added a golden glow to his skin, making it seem to flow all the more smoothly over his lean and sinewed torso.

It was infuriating. He grew all the more attractive, with the hair at his temples and neck now damp and clinging and the shadow of his beard adding to his rugged look. Moreover, by the time he was ready to quit for the day, he was the only one who had expended any nervous energy. Debra felt more keyed up than ever.

Partial solution to the problem came, after Graham had vanished, with a brief running stint down the road near her house. The day's last rays fell across her path in deep ocher shards, warming the air for those last moments before the evening's breeze picked up. Though she'd never been a runner, she had toyed with the idea many times. Now, as she loped along, trying her best to look experienced despite a persistent stitch in her side, she wondered what its devotees ever saw in the sport. It was only when she was back in her loft, having showered and changed into a cool, loose night-gown, that she could appreciate the value of the run. She felt relaxed and comfortably tired. For that, she was grateful. The last thing she wanted was to lie awake half the night rehashing the events of the day. With each thought of Jason's visit, she bristled anew. With each thought of Graham's passion, her pulse quickened. Exhaustion was, indeed, the solution. Her last thought, fresh upon those others just before she fell asleep, was that she might have to become a regular runner, after all.

When a strange car turned in at the drive the following afternoon, she was convinced of it.

Chapter Eight

$\mathcal{I}$t was as strong a sense of déjà vu as Debra had ever experienced. She and Graham were in the house, taking refuge from the sun's heat over cool cans of soda. The phone rang; Debra answered it, then handed the receiver to Graham, who had a brief interchange with the lumberyard clerk before hanging up. He'd barely begun to tell her that the oak treads he'd special ordered had arrived when his gaze shifted to the window.

"You've got a guest," he stated baldly.

She tensed instantly, then sought to deny her fear quickly. "Not me. Maybe it's someone for you?" Her gaze joined his, and her stomach turned over. It hadn't occurred to her that Jason would be back so soon. She'd prayed that he wouldn't come back at all!

Only when the car drew closer did she realize that it wasn't the same. The one Jason had driven had been maroon, while this one was blue. Both bore local plates. Both were driven by a man whose features were more familiar to her with each tire turn. This time, though, Debra burst into a smile of delight as the car came to a full stop and the man inside looked cautiously around.

"It's my father!" she cried in excitement, setting the

175

can on the window sill and bounding out the door. Grinning all the way, she dashed across the yard and threw herself into her father's waiting arms.

"How are you, Debbie?" he asked, holding her tight, then squeezing her a final time before setting her back. "You look marvelous!" He gave her the once over. "No shoes? What's this?"

Swallowing the knot of emotion that had momentarily clogged her throat, Debra dabbed tears of happiness from her eyes. "It's called 'let the toes breathe the country air.' How are you, dad?" Her grin stretched from ear to ear, and she shook her head in disbelief. "What a wonderful surprise!"

David French arched one dark brow into a finely furrowed forehead. With his neatly trimmed salt-and-pepper hair and his well-tailored sport shirt and trousers, he looked as debonair as ever. "I was hoping it would be. I was worried. Jason called me last night all hot and bothered—"

"Jason!" She moaned, then scowled in instantly revived anger. "He didn't lose any time; I can say that for him! He actually called you? Whatever for?"

"He was worried."

"He wasn't worried! He was angry that I dared refuse to go back with him. He was indignant that I told him I didn't love him. And he was jealous."

"Jealous of . . . Graham?" her father asked more softly.

"Yes. Of Graham. My God, Graham's been wonderful to me. If he hadn't been here yesterday, I think Jason might have physically dragged me away. He was impossible!"

"Take it easy now, Debbie." He took her arm and turned her toward the yard. "Let's take a walk and you can tell me about it. Then you can show me this house of yours." He looked around slowly. "You're alone today?"

"No, no," she answered, calming at the thought. "Graham's out back. Come on." She slid her arm from his and took his hand. "I'll introduce you. Then we can sit on the swing and watch him work." She gave an uncommonly innocent smile. "It's a great pastime."

"Does he agree with that?" her father asked chidingly.

"He's never complained. I think he's more at home on that ladder than anywhere else." Rounding the side of the house, the man under discussion came into view. "Graham?" Debra called, leading her father to the foot of the ladder. "I'd like you to meet my father, David French. Dad, this is Graham Reid."

Transferring the hammer to his left hand, Graham descended far enough to extend his right to the older man. "Pleased to meet you, Mr. French."

"The pleasure is mine," the other returned, his keen eyes making an instant analysis that was decidedly favorable. "I've heard a lot about you lately. Between my son and my son-in-law—"

"*Former* son-in-law," Debra interrupted to correct.

"*Former* son-in-law. Thank you, dear. Between the two of them, I'd begun to think that my daughter had hired some kind of brutish monster." There was a devilish gleam in his eye.

Graham smiled, enjoying his candor. "Not quite. I promise you, sir, that I would do nothing to harm your daughter."

With a nod of thanks and leave-taking, the older man linked his arm with Debra's and led her deeper into the yard. As the two settled into the swing out of earshot, Graham returned to work. Yet his thoughts didn't stray far from father and daughter and the happiness that had lit Debra's face when she'd recognized her visitor.

They seemed very close, the two in the swing. Though he couldn't remember hearing much more than a passing mention of her father from Debra, it was obvious that they shared something very special. Tossing a fast glance over his shoulder, he saw Debra sitting sideways on the swing facing her father, holding his hand tucked in her lap. They seemed totally engrossed in one another, their gentle, periodically serious expressions suggesting a warm, caring relationship.

As destructive as jealousy could be at times, Graham felt it now in a most harmless but heart-rending way. He was envious of the relationship Debra had with her father, not in the sense of threatening what *he* might have with her, but rather as a reminder of what he missed with his own daughter, with Jessie.

Mention of her name brought with it a pang of sadness. Her birthday had come and gone, and he'd done nothing to commemorate it. As often as he'd thought to send a card or a gift, he recalled that one time six years ago when she'd sent it back. Somehow he couldn't face that same rejection.

Clamping his teeth against the nails he held in his mouth, he put the full force of his frustration behind his hammer and whammed still another nail into the shingle. Her graduation would be this weekend. This weekend. His daughter graduating from high school. It seemed so hard to believe, but then *he* still pictured the young child he'd known and loved. The young woman was a total stranger, and *that* was even harder to accept than the fact that she'd be off to college in September.

Maintaining a rhythmic hammering, he recalled how he'd talked with his father about giving her a car for graduation. His father had talked with Joan, who had instantly vetoed the idea. *Her* daughter didn't need a car yet, and when she did, *she'd* be the one to buy it for her. Strange, Graham mused, that Joan had always been the more extravagant of the two during their marriage. It was one of the things that had driven them apart; Joan had wanted to lavish every possible luxury on Jessica. Of course, the issue of the car was something else. Joan simply couldn't bear the thought of Graham buying it. Was she threatened? Did mother and daughter have their moments of disagreement? *Did* Jessica ever wonder what it might be like to get to know her father?

It was wishful thinking, he decided as he climbed down the ladder in search of more shingles. She was an adult now. She could have easily contacted him if she'd wanted to. His address was no secret. Lord knew Joan had used it often enough at the start to pen her spiteful little notes. He hadn't heard from her in years. Perhaps she *had* destroyed the page on which his name had been written.

With a deep sigh, he mounted the ladder and positioned another shingle before allowing himself a peek at Debra. She had just that minute torn her eyes from him.

"I can't explain what I feel," she spoke in a near whisper, for her father's ears alone. "I hired him because he was the best carpenter around. I'd looked at what he'd done, and it was exciting. I mean, it's too early for you to see anything here, but I'll show you the plans he drew up and the place he made for me up in the loft. He has a real talent for design. It wouldn't surprise me to learn that he's got an architectural degree stashed away somewhere."

"You haven't asked?"

"Oh, I've tried. But he doesn't like talking about himself. It's not that I feel he's hiding something awful, rather that there's some kind of pain he just doesn't want to face."

David French put a finger against his upper lip and moved it no more than a whisper back and forth. It was his typically pensive gesture. "I checked him out a little."

"You *what?*" Debra cried in dismay. "I thought you were on *my* side!"

"You know I am, Debbie. But I wanted to have plenty of ammunition when either Stuart or Jason calls. They will, you know. I told them I was coming."

She grimaced. "You didn't!"

"I did. I had to calm them down somehow. They're convinced that you're being taken over by this fellow."

"That's absurd. But then, neither Stu nor Jason ever saw me as much of an individual. . . . So, what did you find out about Graham?"

Her father winked. "That everyone seems to like the fellow. He's a hard worker, quiet, private, causes no trouble. I'm sure you were told the same things when you asked."

"Pretty much."

He shifted his gaze from his daughter's face to Graham's more distant form. "They say not to judge a book by its cover, but a cover can often be revealing."

"In what way?" She had her own theory on the matter but was intrigued as always by her father's philosophical streak and his uncanny perceptiveness. She wasn't to be disappointed.

"Though the cover may not tell everything, may even be misleading at times, it can also suggest certain personality characteristics that prove to be accurate. In Graham's case, take his truck for starters. It's clean, well kept. He takes pride in it. Doesn't mess it up with bumper stickers. That says a lot. Suggests he's his own man, doesn't care to broadcast his personal likes and dislikes. He doesn't need people to honk if they play tennis or smile because he has twins. He's not about to ask a stranger whether he's hugged his lawyer today. And he feels no need whatsoever to tell the world whether he loves New York, New Hampshire, Vermont, German shepherds, or Beluga caviar."

Debra burst into soft laughter. "You must have seen a whole load of bumper stickers during the drive up from the airport."

"All passing me on the left. Your father's not as daring a driver as he used to be."

"Thank heavens for that. . . . But, go on."

"About Graham?" When she nodded, he cleared his throat. "His arms are bare."

A giggle bubbled forth. "Of course his arms are bare. So's his chest and his back. It's hot working up there. His shirt's been shading the fence post since midmorning."

"He's got no tattoos."

"No tattoos?" she echoed, entranced. "What does *that* have to do with anything?"

"Well," her father began thoughtfully, "tattoos are like bumper stickers in some respects. Their wearers want to tell the world something. Your Graham doesn't need to tell the world anything. He marches to a different drummer, if you will."

"That could be either good or bad."

"You're right. There are those people who go their own way out of default; they just don't *hear* the beat of the drum. I suspect Graham hears it well enough but has made an active decision to go his own way."

"You're impressed, then?" she asked, trying not to let on how much it meant to her.

If her father saw, he very diplomatically filed the information in the back of his mind. "He's got a direct eye and a firm handshake. Those are good signs." Then he inhaled loudly. "And with that, I'm afraid I've run out of pithy observations. I'd have to spend some time with the man to learn anything more. . . . But, come on." He patted her knee and pushed himself from the swing with a grunt, then turned and held his hand for Debra. "Show me this house of yours. It had better be as good as you say," he warned with a twinkle in his eye that hinted he liked the place already.

Debra took his hand, fully intending to conduct the tour. When they reached the house, though, David French had a new idea.

"Graham!" he called. "Can you spare a few minutes to walk me through your plans? My daughter here is strictly an amateur."

The only problem Debra had with her father's tactic was in restraining the smile that threatened to betray his motive. Still, she made a token protest. "I can show you, dad. Graham is busy—"

"Graham's been busy since I got here. He deserves a break. Are you that harsh a taskmaster?"

The corner of her mouth twitched, fortunately on the side Graham couldn't see. "But he *loves* his work. Can't you hear the devotion behind every stroke of that hammer?"

"Lady and gentleman, please, please . . ." Graham had climbed down from the ladder during the improvisational debate, every bit as curious about David French as the latter was about him. "No arguments on my account," he insisted, easily joining the fray. "I'd be glad to show you around, Mr. French. You're right." He sent Debra a patronizing grin. "Debra may be a brilliant writer, but she's no builder." He lowered his voice in mock gravity as he shifted his gaze to David. "You know how it is with these cerebral types." Then he whispered from the corner of his mouth, the corner on the side Debra couldn't see, "Not very good with their hands."

"I heard that, Graham Reid," Debra argued. "And I take exception. Who built a fire in the fireplace every morning when she first got here?"

"You," he replied docilely.

"Who single-handedly mastered that ancient stove in the kitchen?"

He nodded. "You."

"And who makes you better lunches than two dumb ham and cheese sandwiches in an old brown bag?" At his look of surprise, she eyed him pertly. "I see everything," she drawled, then seized on the momentary advantage. "Now what was that you were saying about my not being good with my hands?"

As clever as she'd thought herself, she'd underestimated her adversary. He scratched his head. "That's funny." He muted a smile. "I was thinking of the blank you drew when it came to getting your bed to the loft. And . . . a scene with a desk and a couple of screws, not to mention a particular roto-tiller . . ."

Debra indulged him his bull's eye for several seconds before turning on her father. "You men are all the same. You pick insignificant points and blow them out of proportion. All right." She threw up her hands. "Go ahead." She looked at Graham. "*You* show him the house, but the carriage house is mine."

"Fair enough," came the smooth, deep reply. Standing back, Graham gestured for her to precede them. She simply mirrored the motion.

"No, no. You both go ahead. I'll just follow a few paces behind in hopes of picking up any pointers that may drift back to me." Her tongue-in-cheek rejoinder was met by a smile from her father, who had remained in the background studying the interchange.

Now he stepped forward and cocked a brow toward Graham. "Lovely child, isn't she?" he mused, sending a final glint over his shoulder before moving toward the house.

Graham simply grinned before taking the lead, while, true to her word, Debra fell to the rear—which happened to be precisely where she wanted to be. It was from that vantage point that she viewed her father and Graham together, that she sensed the instant rapport that seemed to have sprung up between the two.

As they wandered from room to room in the main house, Graham explained both what had been done and what was yet to be done. For every question David raised, Graham had an easy answer. For every follow-up comment Graham made, David had an appropriate response. In some instances, he questioned the plans. Then Graham patiently unrolled the blueprints and painstakingly outlined the rationale behind the particular point. Invariably, David nodded his understanding and agreement.

Debra barely heard the details of what was said; she simply caught the quiet, murmured exchange of words. It warmed her to see that her father was as engrossed in the hearing as Graham was in the telling. That she'd begun to feel like the proverbial woman trailing obediently behind was secondary to the knowledge that with the time spent together, each man would learn more about the other. That mattered very much to her.

So absorbed was she in this more general element of the tour that she was taken off guard when her father suddenly reached back for her hand. "Your turn, Debbie. What's in the carriage house?"

Debra looked from one man to the other. "Uh, you're finished here?"

Graham gave a knowing grin. "We've been through just about everything. I know it must have been boring for you."

His teasing snapped her to life. "Don't believe a word he says, dad. A good half of these ideas were *mine*."

"You mean," her father picked up lightly, "that you actually *did* get something from that college education of yours?"

"No, that's not what I said." She smiled. "For all that

education must have cost, it was really the subscription to *Architectural Digest* you gave me last year that did the trick."

Feigning a look of disgust, David French motioned them forward. "Hmmmph! So much for lofty ideals." Graham's quiet chuckle was left behind as father and daughter made their way around the back of the house to the breezeway, then disappeared into the carriage house.

Retrieving his hammer and nails, Graham was half-way up the ladder before he stopped to realize how much he had enjoyed the exchange with David French. The man obviously knew something about architecture, though Graham couldn't recall Debra's having said what he did for a living. Come to think of it, she'd said very little about him despite frequent discussions about her mother, brother, stepbrother, ex-husband, and producer. He wondered where David fit into the picture of her life and half-suspected him to represent the sane side of the family.

Once more, Graham felt a twinge of envy, though this time it was more direct. Debra loved her father. He couldn't argue with that. What he *could* argue with was a decision she might have made, after the pain she'd suffered at Jason's hands, to restrict her love to tried and true recipients, such as David.

If she never loved again, as a woman should a man, it would be a waste. She had so much to give. Yes, give. He'd been wrong in his initial evaluation of her. More specifically, what he'd wanted to believe just hadn't proved true. From the very start, he'd sensed that she was much more than just a pretty package wrapped up in designer jeans. From the very start, he'd known of his susceptibility to her. Now he was very possibly in love with her, and he wondered at the futility of it.

The irony of it all, he told himself as he struck at

another nail, was that when he was with her, he was no longer the carpenter. When he was with her, he was the successful architect. She made him feel that way. Indeed, so had her father. In their presence, he was the man he'd once been, a man to be consulted, befriended, respected. Debra, in her own persistent way, made him forget how he'd once botched things up. She trusted him, thereby giving him strength. She also inspired feelings in him that made him, for the first time ever, consider trying it all again. As it was, he already dreaded the day when her house would be done, when he'd leave, go to other jobs, face day after day without her. Weekends now were bad enough. He had no idea how he would handle total withdrawal.

The rev of a car's engine cut into his thoughts at nearly the same time Debra's slender form entered his periphery. Graham looked down to find her alone.

"Was that your dad leaving?"

"Uh-huh." She stood at the foot of the ladder with her hands stuffed into the pockets of her shorts. He was only grateful that she wore a shirt today, though how much less sexy it was than the clinging bandeau he wasn't sure. For the sake of comfort, she'd tied its tails into a knot above her waist. The thin band of exposed skin did nothing for his peace of mind, particularly when he allowed himself to recall how soft that particular span of skin was, how soft the skin above it, how ripe the curves above that.

The sharp breath he took could have easily passed for a sigh of regret. "I'm sorry. I would have liked to have said good-by. Will he be back?"

"I don't know. He's thinking of driving farther up into the mountains tonight. That's why he's gone into town—to see about getting some tips from the locals about where to stay. But you'll have a chance to talk with him later. He's invited us to join him for dinner."

She'd purposely couched her words in nonchalance. Now she held her breath, waiting, wondering what Graham would say.

He was taken completely by surprise. "Uh . . . dinner?"

"Uh-huh," she teased in her most coaxing tone. "You know, roast beef and coq au vin and shrimp scampi type of thing?"

He chuckled. "Not up here." Then he caught himself. "On second thought, there *is* one place that's not too bad."

She grinned. "Stonehenge West."

"You've found it already?" He was half-disappointed not to have been able to tip her off to the secret himself.

"Hey, these taste buds were born and bred in New York. Whenever I come within a mile of haute cuisine, I automatically start to drool."

Graham tried his best not to laugh. "That's really disgusting, Debra. I mean, I can picture you driving around in that Blazer of yours, foaming at the mouth, looking frantically for an elusive pocket of urban elegance hidden in the hills." Then he frowned. "How *did* you discover Stonehenge West?"

"You really want to know?"

"Sure." He was game for most anything.

But she paused. "Naw. You'll think I'm crazy."

"Come on. You've got me curious." He turned around and sat back against the ladder, flexing one long leg against a lower rung.

Debra hesitated a minute longer, then began. "Well, you see, I was driving around a couple of weekends ago and found myself on the road behind a beautiful red Mercedes. You know, the 350 SL variety?"

"Do I ever," he murmured, with meaning of his own.

Debra assumed that he shared her admiration of the

vehicle. "It was so odd to see it here. I don't think I've seen one like it in six weeks. Well, I was curious. So . . . I decided to follow it for a bit. You know"—she grinned mischievously—"see where the rich spend their time . . ."

"That *was* a crazy thing to do. You could have found yourself totally lost on some God-forsaken back road with no one around but a well-to-do loony in a pretty car."

"There were a man and a woman in the car. I figured they were going somewhere interesting. Besides, it was no loony at the wheel. He drove very carefully."

"In a 350 SL . . . I should hope so! Okay, what happened?"

She shrugged. "Nothing much, really. I followed them to the restaurant, took a look around and left."

"You saw the rocks?"

"How could I miss them! They're beautiful. Miniatures of the real thing. Even if you couldn't afford the meal, it'd be worth going to the restaurant just for cocktails. The view of the rocks *and* the valley is breathtaking."

"But you can afford the meal. Why didn't you try it?"

She wrinkled her nose. "Oh, I don't know. I wasn't dressed right, for one thing." She looked down at her shorts. "I seem to have forgotten how to wear a skirt."

"And for another thing . . ." he prompted.

"For another thing, I was alone. The joy of a place like that is in sharing it."

Graham felt goose bumps rise on his flesh. Damn, but she had all the right answers! He could only stare at her, feeling himself drawn in more deeply by the minute.

"Will you share it with us tonight, Graham? We'd really like you to."

"Hell, Debra," he replied gruffly. "I'm your carpenter." He struggled to remember it himself. "You don't really want me along while you visit with your father."

"It was his suggestion in the first place," she argued softly. "And, yes, I *do* want you along."

That was all she said, those simple words. Her eyes said the rest. Had she spent five minutes expounding on every possible reason why he should join them, none would have been as eloquent as that direct, if silent, plea. In its wake, he knew he had no choice but to accept.

"We'll need reservations," he cautioned.

"I'm making them now." She crossed to the back door and turned with her hand on the knob. "Is eight too late?" In the city, eight would have seemed early. Here, though, things were different. For all she knew, Graham wolfed down his steak and potatoes before the evening news began. For all she knew, he was asleep before nine.

"Eight's fine," he answered. "If your father's changing here, I can meet you at the restaurant."

The implication was that she'd already have a ride. Debra didn't argue, suspecting that Graham might not relish the thought of fetching her in the pickup. "You're sure you wouldn't like us to stop by and pick *you* up?" she asked, trying to be subtle. She'd love to see where he lived.

It wasn't to be, at least not on this night. "Thanks, but it'll be easier if I meet you there. I'm in the opposite direction, anyway."

"Suit yourself," she remarked with a shrug, then called over her shoulder as she entered the house, "but be there by eight. My father is always punctual!"

So was Graham Reid. In fact, he was early, parking his Mercedes as inconspicuously as possible among the other cars in the small gravel lot, then finding a quiet corner of the lounge in which to nurse a Scotch on the rocks until his host arrived. His host. By rights, *he* should be the host. He could certainly afford it, and these mountains were, in their way, his home. Perhaps he should speak to the maitre d' and have the bill delivered to him at the end of the meal. But no. Debra's father had extended the invitation as a form of hospitality. There'd be a time for reciprocation; he felt it in his bones.

When Debra suddenly materialized beneath the archway, though, what he felt was not in his bones. Taking a hasty swallow of his drink, he rose to meet her.

"You look beautiful," he murmured, enchanted by the vision in white silk offset by a delicate tan, flowing brown hair, dancing eyes and cheeks of the rarest pink. It was all he could do to remember where they were and resist the urge to take her in his arms. After all, they weren't alone. Recalling her father's presence with an abrupt shift of his eyes, he smiled and extended his hand. "Mr. French, good to see you again."

Fortunately for Debra, the men launched into ready conversation, giving her time to gather her wits as she settled into the seat Graham held for her. She'd been stunned on entering the lounge and seeing him. Though she'd known he wouldn't be wearing jeans, none of her imaginings had prepared her for the real thing. Dressed in a navy blazer and light gray slacks, with a white shirt, gray and pink striped tie and loafers, he looked as suave and sophisticated as any patron in the house. His hair was neatly combed and gleamed with the lingering dampness of his shower. Fresh shaven, his skin bore the faintest tinge of a wood-scented balm.

"Something to drink, Debra?" Graham caught her in the act of drinking something far more potent.

Fighting a blush, she jerked her eyes up to the waiter. "Uh . . . a white lillet, please."

The waiter nodded and sought her father's order while Graham tried to recall the last time he'd heard of that particular aperitif. It had been somewhere in the past, somewhere quiet and sophisticated and totally irrelevant to the present. The present . . . the present was Debra. He couldn't seem to take his eyes off her.

The Scotch helped, as did David's genial way of inspiring conversation. By dinner's end, Graham had some thoroughly enjoyable memories to compensate for the frustration of having sat knee to knee with Debra all evening, having watched her talk, eat, smile, having been vitally aware of that soft cleavage that taunted him each time she moved. His feelings were very much mixed when he tucked her into her father's car, thanked the older gentleman and bid the two good night.

Debra's feelings were decidedly darker. "Didn't learn much, did you?" She slanted her father a scowl as he headed the car toward the main road. "He's very careful about what he says. Always the master of evasion. He doesn't give an inch."

"Now, now, Debbie, don't be too hard on him. He must have good reason for wanting to keep his past to himself. Besides, those are simply details. The more important things—his intelligence and integrity—he can't hide."

Gazing into the darkness beyond, Debra sighed. "I guess you're right. It's just . . . frustrating." Frustrating was the word for the night. For as wonderful as it had been to spend the evening with Graham and watch him keep easy pace with her father, it had been pure torture to be so close, yet so far. Even now, she recalled the way his blazer rested comfortably atop his shoulders, making them seem all the more broad, the way the cuff of his white shirt contrasted with the tanned skin of his wrist, the faint sprinkling of tawny hair on the backs of his hands. She recalled how the hair at his nape grazed the collar of his shirt, how his throat graciously accommodated a tie, how his lips thinned a fraction when he caught her staring.

"Are you in love with him, Debra?" Her father's voice cut into her tormented reverie.

"Hmmmmm?"

"You heard me."

She'd also caught his use of her full name, something he did only when he was very serious. "Oh . . . I don't know . . ."

"There's nothing to be ashamed of."

She turned to look at him. "I've been divorced for barely two months! How could I fall in love so quickly? Besides, he's working for me. You don't fall in love with your carpenter."

"Says who?"

"Says *me*," she countered with unexpected vehemence. "That kind of thing is fine for soap opera, not for real life."

Her father's voice softened. "What happens up here isn't exactly soap opera, Debbie. Graham is neither an actor nor a well-to-do playboy fooling around. From what I can see, he's been here, working hard, for eight years. You have to give him credit for that."

"I do, dad. I do! It's just that—well, I have this fear sometimes . . . this fear that there's something else going on with him."

"Another woman?"

"No. Not that."

"Then what?"

She closed her eyes, laid her head against the back of the seat and sighed. "He seems so alone—no family, nothing. It doesn't fit. So *many* things don't fit. He's so open about some things, so closed about others. I do get frightened."

David French drove on in silence for a while, mulling over his thoughts, debating his course. It was only after he'd turned the car in at Debra's drive and come to a stop that he spoke.

"You know," he began gently, turning to face his daughter, "I sat there tonight watching the two of you."

"You were talking."

"I was watching, too. And it seemed to me that you're both trying hard to ignore something pretty obvious."

"Both? Come on, dad. Graham's not about to fall in love with me. He hates city women. He told me so."

"Then he was fooling himself. Because, I'm telling you, he was as aware of you as you were of him. I'm a man. I ought to know." He grinned in the moonlight. "He did a remarkable job, really, carrying on a perfectly calm conversation, all the while feeling your eyes on him." The grin broke into a chuckle. "Remarkable. Really."

Debra scoffed it off. "It wasn't remarkable. He simply wasn't affected by my looking at him."

"Is that why he kept shifting in his seat? Is that why his hand shook when he took a drink? Very slightly . . . but I do notice things like that. Things like the faintest sheen of sweat just above his upper lip—"

"Dad! That's enough! You're being silly!"

Having said what he wanted to say, her father shrugged. "Maybe so. Maybe I'm just hopeful."

"Hopeful of what?"

He grew more sober. "I hate the thought of your being alone up here. You could do worse than Graham."

"Hmmmph," she mumbled. "I did once, and not too long ago. I'd say my judgment isn't worth beans."

"Then listen to your heart."

"My heart! What does my heart know? My heart did me in when it came to Jason!"

"But now you're that much older and wiser. We all have lessons to learn, often the hard way."

Debra missed neither the poignance of his gaze nor the deeper meaning of his words. She, too, remembered those days when they'd never have been able to talk this way. It made their present relationship that much more precious.

On impulse, she leaned over and hugged him. "I love you, dad. You know that, don't you?"

"I do, and believe me, it keeps me going on many a day. Now that Nora's gone . . ." His second wife had died two years before; they'd been happily married for twenty-five years.

"Are you sure you won't stay the night, dad? You could take the bed. I've got a perfectly good sleeping bag."

David French rebounded instantly. "And miss the early golf game I managed to arrange? No, ma'am. The resort is only about an hour from here."

"But it's late. And dark."

"Nonsense. There's a full moon. And I'm a night owl. I'll be fine."

"Will you stop back on your way home?"

He shook his head. "There's a small airport up there. I'll catch a flight to Manchester, then change planes to New York and save myself the drive. But I'll be back soon. When the house is finished I'll come for a week. How does that sound?"

One part of it sounded great. "Is that a threat . . . or a promise?" she teased to cover her dismay at the thought of the house's completion.

"A promise. Now give me a kiss and run inside."

Hugging him soundly, she climbed from the car. Rather than starting for the house, though, she circled around and lingered at his window. "Thanks for coming, dad. It was great. Thanks for . . . everything."

"It was nothing. You take care now. And think about what I said."

"I will," she whispered, then stood back and waved until the car was out of sight. Slowly, she turned and headed for bed.

Sleep was a long time in coming. Neither a long shower nor a cup of warm milk helped. Her thoughts were of Graham and the fact that she was in love with him. Her father had seen it instantly; what point was there in kidding herself? She loved him. She looked forward to greeting him each day, talking with him, watching him work. She felt a comfort when he was around, had come to depend on his understanding when she was confused or upset. And she ached to share whatever it was he kept buried inside, not for the simple sake of knowing but in the hope of helping him deal with something she was convinced pained him.

Her father's words haunted her. *When the house is finished. When the house is finished.* When the house was finished, Graham would have no excuse to come, unless, as her father claimed, he did feel something special for her. Was it all physical? Had what her father seen been nothing more than an intense sexual attraction? From the start, Graham had acknowledged that he wanted her. As for something deeper, she just didn't know.

The hours seemed to drag on endlessly before she finally fell asleep. Then it was to dream of the past weeks and Graham. Time and again, she awoke in a sweat, wondering in the dark what would be when the house was finished. Exhausted by dawn, she finally drifted deeper into sleep, only to bolt back that much farther when the nightmare returned. This time, though, the sun was high in the sky, and Graham himself was leaning over her in concern.

Chapter Nine

*E*yes wide and dazed, Debra stared at him, unsure as to whether she'd imagined him there. When he spoke, she gasped.

"Are you all right, Debra?" he asked, reacting to the look of fright on her face with one of his own. He was propped above her, a hand on the bed on either side of her shoulders. A dark brown T-shirt hugged his chest, faded jeans his hips.

"Oh, Graham!" she whispered, barely blinking, as though afraid he'd disappear if she closed her eyes for that fraction of a second. "It was the same nightmare, over and over. I kept thinking the house was finished . . ." The words came out in a rush, their deeper meaning clear. When she rose spontaneously and coiled her arms around his neck, he held her tight.

It took her several minutes to finally believe he was there, several minutes for the proof of his presence to penetrate her senses. There was the solidity of his chest crushing her breasts, the steel-banded circle of his arms around her back. There was the clean male scent that filled her nostrils and the rapid beat of his heart beside hers. She tightened her grip on his neck, uncaring that she might strangle him, knowing only that she didn't want to let go. A tremor shook her body and reverberated through Graham's.

By some miracle of strength, Graham managed to draw back to look at her, to find the same unbridled yearning on her upturned face that he felt in her pliant body. Fresh from sleep, she was warm and beckoning. Any control he might have had snapped.

Seconds later, their lips met in a fiercely urgent kiss. There was no teasing, no playful tasting and coaxing. There was no slow seduction of one mouth on the other. Rather, there was a raw need that had been two months in the building and now seemed to explode between them. With his hands splayed on either side of her face and his long fingers thrust through the thickness of her hair, he held her face still for the devouring.

Debra held back nothing. She opened her mouth wider to take his plunging tongue in an aggressively erotic prelude that left her breathless. Yet even as she gasped, her own tongue dueled with his, rolling, parrying, reaching for that same dark, moist depth. All the while, her hands surged across his chest, eagerly seeking and spanning the swells of his muscular form, pressing closer, closer to his heat.

On her knees now before him, she felt his restless hands roaming her back. Reaching down, she tugged his T-shirt from his jeans and slid her hands beneath. He released her long enough to whip the shirt over his head and throw it aside before seizing her lips once more.

She was in her glory, touching his chest, rubbing her palms against his flesh, reveling in the heady friction. Her finger tips raked his tawny mat of hair, finding a hidden nipple, bringing it instantly to life. Likewise, Graham's touch was a fire upon her, making her squirm with the inching of her nightgown over her thighs and hips to her waist. His fingers were everywhere, possessing her skin, the curves and hollows that marked her a woman. Their lips clung with a fever while he lifted the gown to her breasts; then he tore himself away to twist it off completely.

A soft sound of aching passion emerged from Debra's throat when she straightened on her knees and brought her naked body forward. Arching her back, she strained closer. She felt the manly roughness of his fingers as they slipped up the back of her thighs, curved over her bottom and conquered her hips. She clutched his head convulsively and held his cheek to her breast. With the slightest inward move, he found her nipple and sucked deeply on it. She cried out mindlessly, feeling enveloped and consumed when he widened his lips and took her in further.

Burying her face in the richness of his hair, she clutched at the bunching muscles of his shoulders. There were moans and intermittent gasps, some from her lips, others from his. When the trembling of her thighs became too great, she settled back on her haunches and offered her lips to his seeking ones. In a moment of shared intent, their hands met at the buckle of his belt, working in a frenzy with each other, against each other, tugging at the belt, then the snap and zipper of his jeans. Moaning his hunger, he nipped her lips and rocked back on his hips to shuck the jeans and his briefs as one. Then he came forward once more, capturing her lips as he pushed her back onto the sun-warmed sheets. With one perfect, breathtaking motion he slid down the frame of her thighs and entered her.

"Graham!" she cried in a ragged whisper, feeling his fullness within her and knowing that nothing had ever been as beautiful. Then all reason fled as he thrust deeper, deeper still, giving her every bit of him, striving to give even more.

The pace was a wild one from the start, the near-savage rhythm of two bodies ideally matched. Graham's strength was endless, each lunge taking them both higher in a grand crescendo that burst at last into a blinding riot of pleasure that left them damp and drained to tumble to reality.

For long moments, the only sounds were those of air being sucked into laboring lungs. Graham's body was heavy on hers, but Debra could barely feel its weight, stunned as she was by the ferocity of his lovemaking. Never in her life had she experienced anything as cataclysmically physical. Never in her life had she ever behaved with such abandonment herself. Their passion had been spontaneous and combustive, both selfish and selfless. It had been truly remarkable.

Eyes closed, she tried to grasp it all. Her arms lay limply on Graham's back, her fingers resting against the dampness of his skin. Then he moaned against her neck and levered himself up. She opened her eyes to find him sitting on the edge of the bed, bent over, his elbows propped on his knees, his hands covering his eyes.

"What is it?" she whispered, sitting abruptly up, suddenly more terrified than she'd been before. If he regretted it, if he hadn't enjoyed it, she thought she'd wither and die right there.

His amber eyes shot to her as if surprised to find her there. Then, his back tensing, he stared straight ahead. Her heart was ready to explode by the time he finally looked back.

"I swore I wouldn't do that," he murmured in self-reproach. His eyes didn't leave her face.

"It was inevitable," she reasoned gently. "You knew that."

"I didn't plan it." He hit his fist against his bare thigh, and she jumped at his vehemence. His voice was little more than a hoarse whisper. "I didn't plan it . . . or I would have brought something."

She raised a hand to his shoulder, then held it back. "Brought something?" she echoed blankly, only slowly beginning to understand. "Something . . . as in birth control?"

When he turned to face her, he wore an expression of gentle urgency. "It was my responsibility, Debra. I did nothing to protect you."

"It's all right," she returned as quietly, eager to put him at ease. "I'm . . . protected." In truth, it was the first thought she'd given the issue in months. During the trauma of the divorce, it simply hadn't occurred to her to advance her yearly gynecological appointment for the purpose of ridding herself of a protection she'd not intended to need.

Graham felt a surge of relief, then a twinge of regret that unsettled him. His thoughts had been of the past, of Jessica's conception and the marriage that had necessarily followed. But Debra wasn't Joan. The thought of Debra bearing his child warmed him. His expression slowly softened, and he lifted a hand to her face in wonder, captured in her spell once more.

"I didn't hurt you, did I?" he whispered.

Debra smiled and shook her head, touched by the concern of such a large, physical man. The memory of his vibrant possession brought a delicate blush to her cheeks. "I love you, Graham," she whispered. "You know that, don't you?" Lifting a hand, she finger combed the hair from his brow. His own hand fell to rest against her neck, his thumb at her pulse, lightly caressing. The amber of his eyes was as warm as the sunlight spilling in from above.

"I think I knew you wouldn't give yourself to me unless you did." Leaning forward, he touched his lips to hers softly, tenderly. "I love you, too, you know."

"I didn't," she murmured against his lips, "but I'm glad." With a sigh, she surrendered to the sweet ardor of his mouth. She closed her eyes in delight, only to jerk them open a second later when a distant sound broke the silence.

"The phone," she whispered.

"Mmmmmm." He was too busy tasting the goodies he'd wolfed down earlier to speak.

"Should I answer it?"

"Uh-uh." He shook his head to make his point, then drew his head back. "You're beautiful, Debra," he murmured thickly, dropping his eyes for the first time to her body. "Very soft." She felt his gaze on her breasts, her waist, her hips, branding her his. Then he reached out to touch what he'd claimed, trailing his fingers in a figure eight around her breasts, then lower to her navel, and lower still until she caught her breath and swayed toward him.

In one deft move, he took her in his arms and twisted, falling back to the bed with her on top of him. This time, their lovemaking was slow and sensual, a leisurely savoring of what had been missed in the frenzy before. If he'd been the man of the flesh, the carpenter, then, he was now the skilled and subtle artist. Debra's whole body swelled to his touch, from her heart on out.

This time, there were soft words of love to enrich their joining. When, side by side, their bodies heated, then tensed, then merged into one, they knew a total meshing of minds and hearts that made their final ecstasy all the more magnificent.

It was nearly noon before they finally pulled each other out of bed. The phone had rung several times; without compunction, they'd let it ring. Arm in arm, wearing nothing at all, they walked through the breezeway into the house to shower. Then, with towels draped appropriately, they feasted on a belated breakfast of bacon and eggs and blueberry muffins before feasting on each other once more.

"Not a very good day for work," Graham quipped, lying propped against the headboard with Debra propped against him. While he admired the view of the loft from the bed, she admired the view of his body from his chest. But the thought of work tore her from her play.

"Oh, Lord. What time is it?" Twisting to look across at the clock radio, she jumped up and turned on the television. "Sorry, Graham," she kidded, scrambling back on the bed and snuggling up to him. "It's either this . . . or the shingles. You choose."

She felt his laughter against her ear, a deep masculine sound that pleased her. Reaching down, he cupped her bare bottom and pressed her close for a last minute. "I choose you, but since you're otherwise occupied, I'd better see to the walls." Shifting to tip her unceremoniously onto the bed, he stood up and retrieved his clothes. By the time he was dressed, the first segment of "Love Games" was underway. Leaning forward, he caught Debra unaware, kissing the tip of her breast before straightening and heading for the house.

An hour later, she followed, feeling bright and buoyant and vibrantly alive. Seeing Graham on the ladder in back, she smiled brightly. "How about something cool?"

"Sounds good."

She'd no sooner set foot inside the house when the phone rang. This time, she couldn't ignore it. Trotting to the living room, she scooped up the receiver.

"Hello?"

"Debra, it's Stuart. Where in the devil have you been? I've been trying your number all day!"

She was high enough on love to overlook his unwarranted indignation. "I've been busy. What's up?"

The voice on the New York end grew smug. "I've finally dug something up."

"Dug something up? On what?"

"On *whom*. Graham Reid."

She stiffened, but Stuart had no way of knowing. He raced on, proud of himself.

"I happened to mention his name to John LeDuc. You remember John, don't you? LeDuc and Sons Construction? He's one of the sons. Anyway, during the discussion, he asked for you. I told him what you were planning up there with your house and that you'd hired a fellow to do the work. When I mentioned Reid's name, he thought it sounded familiar. Called me back just a little while ago." He paused for a breath and to take in the silence on the other end. "Debra, are you there?"

"I'm here," she replied more softly, torn between wanting to hear what Stuart had learned and wishing only for the status quo. She loved Graham *without* any knowledge of the past. As her father had said, the past was nothing but detail. She knew all that was truly important.

Stuart disagreed. "He lived in New York. Did you know that?"

She hadn't, though she wasn't surprised. If not New York, it would have been another cosmopolitan city. She'd always recognized an urbanity about him. "He was an architect," she stated calmly, fitting that piece to the puzzle herself.

"You knew?" Stuart asked, deflated.

"Yes," she replied quietly, then tried to sound marginally bored. "Tell me what else you learned."

"He has a degree from Columbia. Even before he graduated, though, he married the daughter of a banker. A very wealthy banker. The marriage produced a daughter."

All thought of nonchalance vanished, taking Debra's breath with it. A daughter? He'd never mentioned a child! But then, he'd never mentioned this past. "*Had* a daughter?" she heard herself ask.

"Oh, she's still around, I assume. Rumor has it, though, according to John, that Reid hasn't been back to New York since the split. And that was a long time ago."

She did know that. It fit in with his disdain for city women. So . . . his wife was a wealthy city woman. It must have been an ugly divorce. And he had a daughter. . . .

"What do you think, Deb?"

She thought that Graham should have told her all this. But he hadn't. All she could do was to hope that at some point he would. "What am I supposed to think, Stuart? Is this information supposed to be earth shattering? Graham is my carpenter. I don't care about his personal history. What matters is whether he can do the job—" With the appearance of Graham at the door, she broke off her words. How much he'd heard of the conversation, she didn't know. But his eyes were glued to her face and the stricken expression she wore. It was with great effort that she eased it and produced the semblance of a smile. Then she averted her eyes.

"Anything else, Stuart?" she asked quietly.

"No. . . . He did have an excellent reputation as an architect."

It was quite a concession for Stuart to make. "Thank you for saying that. . . . Is everything else okay?"

"Yes." He paused, then ventured a more cautious "Did dad get up there?"

"Uh-huh. Yesterday."

"Have a nice visit?"

"Uh-huh." She had no intention of elaborating.

"Well, I just thought you should know about—"

"I do. Thanks again. Bye-bye, Stuart."

The phone was resting comfortably on its cradle before Graham spoke. "Any problem?"

"No, no. No problem." She scrambled to her feet and headed for the kitchen. He caught her arm and pulled her gently against him.

"No problem?" he murmured. "Then why won't you look at me."

She raised her eyes slowly. "I'm looking at you," she whispered, feeling a strange hurt even as his closeness melted her. Her gaze fell to his lips, which promptly lowered to meet hers. The kiss was tentative but sweet. With a helpless sigh, she relaxed against him.

"That's better," he murmured, and straightened. "Now, how about that drink?"

She smiled. The past *didn't* matter. "Right." Taking his hand, she led him to the kitchen, where she made a pitcher of fresh lemonade. They drank it on the swing in back, with Graham sprawled lengthwise and Debra snug between his knees leaning back against him. It was a quiet time, a lazy time. Stuart's phone call seemed an age away, until the phone rang again. She stiffened instantly.

Graham's arm tightened below her breasts. "Let it ring."

"I can't."

His breath fanned her cheek. "You did before."

"I know." She sat up and laid a hand on his chest. The steady beat of his heart was a comfort. "That's why I can't now." Pushing herself up, she started toward the house. "Stuart was pretty annoyed when he couldn't get through," she called over her shoulder. "This may be someone else with the same problem."

Reaching the phone on the run, she answered it breathlessly. "Hello?"

"Debra?"

"Mother! How are you?"

"I'm fine. Are *you* all right? You sound faint."

"Just out of breath. I had to run in from the back yard. How're things?"

Lucy Shipman proceeded to outline "things," which happened to be a new dress she'd ordered for the fiftieth birthday party of one of her friends. No word was spoken about her own wedding; Debra knew it was on temporary hold. What Debra didn't know was that her mother had another reason for calling.

"I talked with Stuart this morning."

"Oh?" She grew alert, instinctively wary.

"It's quite a coincidence, really. Mildred knows this Reid fellow of yours."

"Mildred?"

"You know Mildred, darling. She's—"

"Of course, I know Mildred." She happened to be the biggest gossip in Lucy Shipman's crowd. "But how did Mildred come to be consulted?" Debra shot back in annoyance.

"Well, Stuart called me and told me that Graham had once lived in New York, and naturally I was curious. If he was *anybody*, Mildred would have heard of him."

Debra scowled. "Obviously, he was *somebody*."

"Oh, yes. His wife was Joan Yarrow. Her father is—"

"I know, mother."

The older woman went on, oblivious to the note of impatience in her daughter's voice. "Graham had no money to speak of. His father was a schoolteacher and just managed to get his sons through college. There were two of them, Graham and another." She took a breath. "Anyway, it was his wife's money that got him started. He had his own architectural firm. After the marriage fell apart, he stayed in New York a while, then left and hasn't returned."

Debra took a steadying breath. "Your Mildred *is* a storehouse of knowledge, isn't she?"

"Now, now, dear. Sarcasm is unnecessary. You may have already known all this, but I didn't. And the *pièce de résistance* is yet to come."

"The daughter."

"How did you know?"

Debra couldn't get herself to confess that she'd learned it from Stuart. "I've known the man for two months, mother. We do talk every so often."

Her mother's voice lowered in eager conspiracy. "Does he ever mention her—this Jessica? From what Mildred hears, they're very much estranged. Pity, too, especially since it was a shotgun wedding to begin with. You'd think that if a man wanted the child enough to marry the mother, he'd insist on visitation rights. But then," she prattled on, "the girl is quite grown up. She's just graduated from high school."

Stunned, Debra slid to the floor and sat cross-legged, slouched over the phone. "I'm sure there are reasons," she murmured softly as she struggled to assimilate the information her mother had so gleefully passed on.

"Well, find them out, darling. It's a terrific story. Maybe you could even use something like that on your show. By the way, I watched the show yesterday, and I thought it was great. Was that your script?"

It was all Debra could do to hear the rest of her mother's chatter, much less respond to it. Relieved when it finally ended moments later, she hung up the phone and crumbled back against the wall. Why couldn't *he* have told her? Didn't he trust her enough?

A daughter named Jessica. A high school graduate. The *raison d'être* of a marriage that had gone on to fail, anyway. At least it explained his concern that Debra be protected against pregnancy. He'd been through a forced marriage once. But marriage wasn't the issue here. Or was it?

"Debra?" Graham's voice echoed from the kitchen through the open rooms of the house.

"Right here," she called weakly, then looked up to find that her eyes had flooded with tears. She was in the process of brushing them away when he appeared.

Taking one look at her sitting in a small, sad bundle

on the floor, he cocked his hands on his hips and glowered. "Damn! They did it again! Who was it this time? Harris . . . Mike?" His eyes darkened all the more. "It wasn't Jason, was it?" Crossing the room in several long strides, he held a hand out to pull her up.

"No," she sniffled through an embarrassed smile, "it wasn't Jason." On her feet now, she looked at Graham, then away. "It was my mother." Freeing her hand from his, she walked to the window. Quite unexpectedly, she felt a surge of anger. It was *his* fault this time. *Graham's.* If he'd been forthright with her, nothing either Stuart or her mother had said would have hurt her.

"Is anything wrong?" Graham asked from where he stood, acutely aware of the distance she'd put between them.

She shook her head. "Just the usual . . . chatter."

"Maybe you should get an answering device."

Debra twirled around. "She's my mother, for God's sake! I can't put her off with something like that!"

"Take it easy, Debra. It was only a suggestion."

He was right. And she knew she was overreacting. Somehow she couldn't help herself. When the phone rang by Graham's foot, she glared at it.

He stooped down. "I'll get it—"

"*I'll* get it!" she retorted in her most imperious tone, angry brown eyes daring him to defy her. He didn't, though he didn't move, remaining on his haunches within inches of her. "Hello!" she barked into the phone, standing up and turning her back on Graham.

"Deb? Is that you?"

"It's me, Harris." She wasn't in the mood for this one any more than she'd been for the other two. More accurately, it had been the other two that soured her day. No, it had been Graham. But this morning had been so beautiful . . .

"Is everything all right?" Harris asked innocently enough.

Debra threw up a hand in aggravation. "Why is everyone always asking me that? Of *course* everything's all right."

"You sound like you're ready to kill."

"Not kill. Maim, perhaps. It's one of those days." She sighed. "What's doing there?"

"Uh . . . maybe I should get you another time."

"You've got me now. Go ahead." She was vaguely aware of Graham rising to his full height behind her. Still, there was silence on the other end of the line. "Harris, what is it?"

"It's Jason."

She grew instantly cold. "What about him?" Graham came to stand before her. When she made a half-turn, he reached out and held her arms. Though she could easily have moved away, she needed his strength right then.

"He was furious when he got back from seeing you. Debra, he's demanding I let you go." She shuddered, and Graham gently rubbed her upper arms. "I mean, it's absurd. What's going on with you two?"

"Nothing. We're divorced."

"That's what I thought. So what's he doing chasing after you to New Hampshire? He blew in here incensed this morning. He claims that the situation is untenable, that you're determined to torment him. What are you doing, Deb?"

"Nothing. He wants me back, and I refuse. That's it."

"He's impossible here. I don't know what to do."

"You could fire me," she dared, disgusted enough at that moment to care less.

Harris quashed the possibility with a laugh. "And lose the most reliable writer I've got? No way! It's

Jason who's missing deadlines right and left. What can I do about *him?*"

"I don't know, Harris. I just don't know."

There was a pause. "Do you think you could . . . try to talk with him?"

She gave a bitter laugh. *"Me? Talk with Jason? We had one hell of a scene up here the other day."* Her voice rose in anger. "It's not my talk Jason wants. It's total obedience." When her breathing faltered, Graham tightened his grip on her arms. "Well, I've had it with being Jason's lap dog. I'm sorry, Harris. He's your problem now."

"You're sure there's nothing—"

"What can I say to him? Jason, behave yourself? Jason, let go? Jason, grow up? Don't you see, Harris? It's something Jason's going to have to work out himself. I have."

Her final words gave Harris pause. "You have, haven't you? Since you've been there, your scripts are better than ever." Then he sighed. "Okay, Debra. Sorry I bothered you. I just thought it was worth a try."

"Harris—"

"Yes, doll?"

"Uh . . . be patient with him. He's a gifted writer."

"Believe me, if I didn't know that, I'd have canned him two weeks ago. You think I like what he's doing around here? He's got my leading ladies at each other's throats—" He caught himself, recalling Debra's hurt. "Sorry about that, doll. Well"—he sighed—"I'll give him a little longer. I owe him that much."

"Thanks, Harris."

"Don't thank me. You just keep sending me your best. I need you, Deb."

"Thanks."

For whatever relief she might have felt at learning that her job was safe, Debra felt an abundant surge of frustration at knowing that so little else was right. Hanging up the phone, she slipped from Graham's grasp and replaced the instrument on the floor.

"I'd better go do some work," she murmured, and tried to sidestep him. He stopped her.

"What was that all about?"

"Nothing." If he didn't see fit to share his life with her, why should she share hers?

"It was Harris. Jason's giving him trouble."

"It's nothing."

"Debra . . ." His voice held warning. When she simply stared past him, he took her chin in the crook of his hand and turned her face to his. "What's wrong, Debra?"

Had he held her hurtfully or growled at her, she might have been able to resist. But his fingers were gentle, his voice soft. And his gaze plunged straight to her heart. To her dismay, her eyes filled with tears once more.

"Oh, Graham . . ." she began in a broken whisper, only to be interrupted by the harsh peal of the phone.

Both pairs of eyes flew downward. When the sound came again, Graham made his decision. Taking her hand, he headed for the door. "Come on. We're getting out of here."

"Graham, what . . . ?"

After making sure the front door was locked, he led her through the house to the back, locked its door as well, did the same for the carriage house, then put her in his truck.

Sensing something about to happen, Debra didn't speak. Glancing at Graham from time to time, she saw a tension in his face that could not have been caused by her phone calls alone. He drove silently, acclimating himself to the course he'd chosen.

They drove northward, toward the mountains.

When, after a half hour, he turned the truck from the main road onto a more rustic one, she had an inkling of their destination. When a beautiful home, a contemporary structure built in against the hillside, came into view, she was sure.

"This is yours, isn't it?" she whispered.

"My home. Yes." He parked the truck beneath a stand of towering pines and came around to help her out.

"You built it yourself?"

"Yes."

She walked slowly to the front of the house, awed by its magnificence. Not large, it was imposing nonetheless, with a frame of redwood, a high, sloping roof and an endless front expanse of glass. She was entranced. "It's just like you, you know."

"Like me?" he asked with returning humor. They stood side by side; she tipped her head to look up at him.

"Uh-huh. It's cleverly hidden away, disguised by a rural road and a veil of trees. But it's got style and sophistication. It's different from anything else around."

The look he cast her was keen and somber. "Different can be either good or bad. Same for style and sophistication."

"I love the house, Graham," she said meaningfully. Then, reaching out to slip her hand in his, she asked more softly, "Why did you bring me here?"

"I wanted you away from that phone. It's far more upsetting than it's worth!"

"But why *here*? We could have gone for a ride, could have spent the afternoon somewhere else."

It was his moment of truth. He could still steer her from the house, take her walking in the woods, then take her out to dinner—all without setting foot in the house. He recalled the first time he'd been to her place, when he'd been so hesitant to take that final step across the threshold. But it had been fated. As was this.

Holding her hand more tightly, he led her up the walk and into the house, guiding her through the main rooms, ending at last in his den. There he released her and walked to the desk, staring for a minute at the photographs before turning and sinking heavily against its edge. Debra had no time to look around. Her eyes never left Graham's face. By instinct alone, she knew that this room represented all he'd left behind.

"My wife's name was Joan," he began with quiet deliberation. "We met when I was still in school. She was several years behind me. We, well, we had a good time together. We were carefree"—his expression grew progressively clouded—"irresponsible, shortsighted. She became pregnant, so we married. I got my degree in architecture several months later. Several months after that, our daughter was born."

Leaning sideways, he lifted her picture. Debra came closer to see. "Jessie. Jessica." He let the frame fall to his knee. "I adored her. So did Joan. Unfortunately, that was the only thing we shared as time passed. The marriage was a dismal failure."

"Why, Graham?"

He shrugged and looked down. "It was really very simple. She came from wealth; I didn't. To me, it was a luxury; to Joan, a necessity. Some of the things that made me the happiest didn't cost a cent—walking in the park on an autumn Sunday, spending time at home playing with Jessie. As for Joan, well, Joan needed more glamour, more glitter. We grew further and further apart. I didn't like her choice of restaurants; she didn't care for mine. I didn't like her vacation plans; she didn't care for mine. I didn't like her friends; she didn't care for mine. And Jessie was stuck right in the middle, being torn in half."

Seeing the pain on his face, Debra ached for him. Stepping between his knees, she curved her fingers around his thighs in a gesture of warmth without seduction. Her eyes bid him continue. She said nothing to break his pace.

"I was able to establish my own firm in New York, thanks to Joan's money. She never let me forget that. But I did well. The firm was quite successful." He paused to frown. "That was one of the problems. By the time I'd repaid her investment and then some, I had developed some very strong ideas about what I wanted to do with our lives. For the first time, I felt I had the right to a say. I could afford just about anything I wanted, with money *I'd* earned."

He inhaled deeply and looked off to the side, his expression one of resignation. "Things came to a head very soon after that. By the time we agreed to the divorce, we were barely talking. Joan took just about everything we'd had; after all, they were her things. I moved into an apartment across town. Jessie was to be with me every other weekend."

His gaze fell, and he grew silent. Debra felt his absence, knew he was reliving that time. Wanting to share it with him, she lightly ran her hands along the outsides of his thighs, desperate to bring him back to her. He returned slowly, his voice soft and haunted.

"It wasn't that bad at first. I planned all kinds of fun things for us to do. She seemed to enjoy being with me. She was seven then. By the time she was eight, it was harder; by the time she was nine, even worse. Each time I saw her, she was more of a stranger to me. Then she began to resist going with me, either claiming some other plans or simply crying." He raised his eyes to hers in pleading. "How could I fight her? She seemed so miserable. A little girl *should* be able to do things with her friends on weekends. And it seemed only natural that she'd grow more awkward with me as she grew up—or so I reasoned. It was only when she became outwardly belligerent, when she inadvertently blurted things out, that I realized Joan was feeding her negative images of me."

"And there was nothing you could do?" Debra blurted out, feeling his frustration as if it were her own.

"What *could* I do? Sure, I spoke with Joan. She denied any wrongdoing. And I had no proof other than a ten-year-old's ranting about what her mother had said. Could I go into court and put the child on the stand? And even if she'd told the truth, what good would it have done? Could I really demand custody of a child who simply didn't want to be with me?"

Debra offered a softer "No. Of course, you could not."

"I would have tried for custody at the start, had it not been for three things. Joan was a good mother, she loved Jessica, and Jessica obviously adored her. I was the odd one out." His words died off in defeat with a finality that shook Debra.

"Was that when you left New York?"

He nodded. "I had always had this dream of living in the country. It seemed a perfect solution."

"But your work . . . your firm. What happened?"

He shrugged. "I closed shop."

"Just like that?"

"It was easy enough. I had several partners by that time. They bought me out. I had plenty of money of my own, and I'd made several wise investments. So I came up here and bought this land."

"You didn't miss the work?"

Graham smiled gently. "I still *had* the work. In many ways, it was more exciting than ever. Not only could I design, but I could build. As a kid, that was what I'd always loved doing. Granted, the scope of my projects is smaller here. I'm not about to put up a concrete and steel skyscraper with my own two hands. But I do feel

happier, more satisfied, than I ever did in New York."
He smiled. "I guess it's the animal in me needing a
physical outlet."

"Some animal," Debra teased softly. Raising a hand
to stroke his cheek, she felt as close to him as she'd ever
been to another human being. "I can't decide whether
it's a lion or a pussycat. You *are* an enigma at times."

All teasing gone, he eyed her somberly. "That's
because I haven't been as open with you as I should
have been. It's because there are times when I feel like
a total failure and I don't know how to cope."

"Failure?" She knew precisely to what he referred.
"How can you say that? You tried, Graham. For two,
no, three years, you tried your best."

"But did I?" he asked with a sharpness that pierced
her, giving her a sample of how he must have tormented himself over the years. "Or did I take the coward's
way out? I could have been firmer with Jessie and
insisted that she spend the time with me. Maybe I gave
in too easily. Maybe she came to believe I just didn't
care enough to fight her. Maybe that's what drove her
away."

Debra shook her head. "No, Graham. I know you.
You're warm and giving."

"I can also be gruff and troubled."

"At times, only at times. And the other is always
right there, ready for a quick comeback."

"But maybe Jessie only saw the angry side. Maybe I
frightened her off. Each time I picked her up, she'd
either be all teary-eyed or in a temper. It'd upset me
instantly. God only knows what I was like in her eyes!"
The depth of his torment was written all over his face.
Debra wanted nothing more than to hold him, to rock
him, to make things better. But the solution wasn't that
simple.

"What happened after you moved here? Did you see
her at all?"

"I tried. I had my dad bring her up several times—by some miracle, *their* relationship remained intact. But she was always withdrawn and unhappy. I finally gave up and resorted to simply sending her notes and cards." His voice shook with emotion, yet it was Debra's throat that grew tight. "After a while, she didn't bother to read them. When one actually came back unopened, I just stopped. She seemed to be coping with the divorce by totally denying my existence. I tried to do the same." He gave a snort of disgust. "Unfortunately, it didn't work."

From amid a deafening silence, Debra tried to find the words to sum it all up. "You have no contact with her, then?"

"None. I haven't seen her in over seven years."

Debra looked down at the photograph he'd dropped on the desk. "She's a beautiful girl."

His eyes joined hers in admiration of the fair-haired, smiling high school graduate. "Yes."

"Have you ever thought to try it again? Now that she's older, she might be more open."

"Naw. I'm no glutton for punishment. It's one thing to think of her as a child, being hurt and angry and blinded to the truth. It's another thing to see her as an adult who may be every bit as bitter and narrow-minded as her mother."

Debra raised both hands to his shoulders in entreaty. "But you don't know that! For all you know, she may be much more of her own person now. She may have enough courage to stand up to her mother and view you with an open mind."

His gaze narrowed. "I've thought of that possibility on occasion. But if that were the case, why hasn't she contacted me? I haven't gone anywhere. I'm exactly where I was when she last saw me. So why hasn't she called, written, come?"

"Maybe she's afraid. That happens sometimes, you

know. There's this mutual fear of being hurt. All it takes is for one person to take the first step—"

"Come on, Debra. That's starry-eyed idealism if I've ever heard it."

Her eyes held his unwaveringly. "It worked for me."

Embroiled in the argument, Graham opened his mouth to further his point when her words sank in. He closed his mouth and stared at her, then frowned. "What?"

"I said, 'It worked for me.'"

"What did?"

"Taking that first step."

"What are you talking about, Debra?"

"My father and I."

It was as though she were speaking a foreign language. "Your father and you?" He tipped his head in puzzlement. "Explain."

She did so, but very softly. It wasn't something she liked to discuss. In this case and with this man, though, the time was right. "Would you believe that there were many years when I didn't know my father?"

"No, I wouldn't," he rejoined vehemently. "You and David have a perfectly delightful relationship, one of the most natural I've ever seen between father and daughter."

"Looks that way, doesn't it?" She gave a satisfied smile.

"You mean it's not true?"

"Oh, it's true. But it wasn't always like that. For the first fifteen years of my life, I didn't know him at all."

"I don't believe you."

"You'd better, since it's fact. My parents were divorced within a year of my birth. Mother remarried within a year after that; dad just seemed to disappear."

"What do you mean . . . disappear?"

"He just wasn't there. Wasn't around."

"Didn't he visit?"

"He may have at first, but I was too young to notice. By the time I knew anything, he was out of the picture."

"But why? How can a man leave a child—two children—like that?"

"Men—people—do strange things when they're threatened," she explained gently, much as her father had explained when at last they'd reconciled. "In the case of my father, he'd found my mother a little more than he could handle. She is a character; there's no other way to put it. He just didn't want to try to keep up with her. You've met him. He's a genuine, easygoing fellow. Those are two words that one doesn't often use in describing my mother. And I'm not being critical, simply honest. Mother is a very lovable flake."

"Debra . . ." Graham chided, his voice deep and extremely soft.

"I'm serious. I do love her . . . for what she is. Dad couldn't do that. So he left. As the years passed, he wanted to contact us. But with each year, he felt he had that much less of a right."

"And you? Were you feeling anything about him during that time?"

She heard the intense interest in his voice and felt a kind of elation. He had to believe there was hope.

"I was curious. From the time I was ten, perhaps, I wondered what he was like. My mother handled it well by explaining that he had his own life, that he'd married again and was happy. But she also let slip that he came to New York often on business. I began to fantasize about what it would be like to bump into him in a restaurant and discover who he was."

"What finally did happen?"

She grinned. "I bumped into him in a restaurant and discovered who he was."

Graham eyed her skeptically. "You've got to be kidding."

"No. I really did run into him. By accident, of course. I was making a beeline for the ladies' room the way fifteen-year-old girls have a way of doing. I rounded a dark corner and ran into him."

"But how did you know it was him?"

"I didn't. He knew it was me. He'd seen pictures all along, the last of which had been taken only two or three months before. When he couldn't stop staring at me, I got frightened and ran back to the table. He could have just left; he was sitting in a totally different room. But he took that step and followed me. Mother, being in a particularly whimsical mood, introduced us readily."

"And that was it? You were buddies from that moment on?"

"Not exactly. In fact, he called three times before I finally agreed to talk with him. I was frightened and angry. But that other need was greater."

"Which one?"

"The one to know the man whose genes are mine."

For a long time, Graham simply stared, his expression one of utter disbelief. "And you really grew as close as you are after having been separated all that time?" he asked at last.

"I think that in some ways the closeness has come as a result of the separation. Many people take family relationships for granted. We didn't. We do subtle things at times, little things, as if to make up for the years we were apart. For example, he always calls me Debbie. I'm sure there's reason for that. And when I'm with him, one part of me *does* feel like a kid again. But only one part. Dad accepts me as an adult. He gives me room, never crowds me. And I can treat him the same way without fear of losing him. After all, he did take the first step that day in the restaurant."

Graham shook his head in slow amazement. "I can't believe it. The two of you seemed so close."

"We are . . . *now*. But it took a while."

"And there's a message here for me?"

"Only that it *can* happen. It may not for you. There's no way to tell. But you have to realize that your problem isn't unique any more than it's unsolvable."

He took a breath that raised his shoulders up and back in a gesture of hope. "And *you* don't think any less of me . . . knowing all this?"

She eyed him as though he were crazy. "Think less of you? How could I, Graham?"

"You could blame me for blowing it as a father."

"You did your best in an untenable situation. What more could anyone ask?"

A gentle hissing sound escaped his lips. "You're unbelievable, do you know that?" He slipped his hands around her waist and clasped them together at the small of her back. "I mean, nothing at all has changed, but I feel relieved. That was the first time I've told anyone about Jessie. It's as though you've lifted a burden from my shoulders."

Her heart swelled. "Only half a burden. It's called sharing the load."

Graham gathered her in his arms then and held her tight. A tremor passed through him, accompanied by a moan. "I love you," he whispered. "I do love you."

Feeling warm and fulfilled, she smiled against his neck. "I hope so," she murmured. "I'd hate to be the only one to carry *that* load."

He pulled back to slant her a crooked smile. "A burden, is it?"

Her insides melted. "You bet! But it's not on the shoulders."

"No?" he growled. "Then where?"

She put her hand to her heart. "Here."

"Here?" he teased, pushing her hand aside and closing his own around her breast.

It was all uphill from there. A touch became a caress

222

that inspired kisses of increasing intensity. When Debra finally caught her breath again, she was beside Graham in his large oak bed, spent and satisfied, covered by nothing but the fine sheen of sweat that their lovemaking had induced. It was a glorious moment, as was the one after and the one after that, a glorious night all told. When, the next morning, they returned at last to her house, her thoughts were all of a future with Graham.

Then the phone rang, and her future crumbled.

Chapter Ten

I don't believe you," she snapped indignantly, unsettled by the confidence in Jason's voice.

"It's true, Debra. The divorce isn't legal."

"Why not?" Her fingers tightened convulsively around the receiver.

Alarmed by the pallor of her face, Graham came up to her side. "What is it?" he whispered with quiet urgency. But she held up a hand, needing to hear Jason's every word.

"My signature . . . the permission I gave for the divorce?" Jason prompted.

"What about it?"

"It wasn't properly notarized. The man had let his certificate lapse. The seal was outdated."

"That can't be!" Debra cried, unwilling to let him wrench happiness from her this way. "You're trying to trick me, Jason. *Why?*" Graham reached for her arm in support. She closed her fingers around his and held on for dear life.

"It's no trick, sweetie," Jason replied in a tone just short of gleeful. "I told you I wanted you back with me. You have no excuse now. You're still my wife."

Chilled, she began to tremble. The thought of being married to Jason, now that she'd come to know and love Graham, was anathema. "I'll never be your wife again, Jason! If necessary, I'll go right back to Haiti a second time!"

"Without my consent?" Jason jeered. "You haven't got a case. No lawyer will make the arrangements if you don't have my agreement. And I have no intention of making that mistake twice."

"You signed willingly enough the first time."

"I wasn't in my right mind then. I am now."

Debra raised tear-filled eyes to Graham and bit her bottom lip. "I'll fight you, Jason. I'll take you to court. You'll be the one accused of adultery. Is that what you want?"

"You have no proof."

"No proof?" she shrieked. "The whole set knew what was going on. Any one of them will testify on my behalf!"

"Will they?" Jason countered smugly. "And take the chance of being canned? I'm pretty powerful around here."

"Not as powerful as you think! *I'm* still on the roster."

Jason gave a snort. "You? Ach, that's just because you've got Harris half in love with you. But you won't have him. And you certainly won't have your goon of a handyman. I'll see to that."

Her voice wavered as the pressure within her mounted. "What are you talking about?"

"A contested divorce can drag on for years, Deb. It can be very messy and very public."

"But you're the wrongdoer! You'll be the one raked over the coals!"

Undaunted, he spit back with a venom that turned her chill to ice. "I'll claim that you were deficient, Debra, that you denied me both conjugal rights and satisfaction. I'll claim that I had good reason to seek someone else. Is that what you want? Is *that* what you want the world to hear . . . that your only sexual outlet is in the scripts you write!"

"That's vile!" Debra cried, on the verge of breaking down. "It's vile and untrue! You can't do this, Jason! I won't let you!"

As distraught as her voice was, Jason's was dangerously calm. "I'll do it, Debra. Think about it. I want you here with me, and I won't stand for much more of a delay. You can't choose someone else, honey. I'm your husband."

"We'll see about that!" she wailed, and slammed down the phone moments before she burst into tears.

Graham's arms were around her instantly, offering a warmth to her chilled body. "It's all right," he crooned, pressing her head to his chest even as he struggled to control his own anger. Having heard enough of the conversation to get its gist, he was livid. "Shhhh. It's all right, Debra."

"But it's not!" she said, sobbing, her words muffled against his shirt. "He's a spoiler! He doesn't . . . care about anything but himself! My feelings . . . mean *nothing* to him! My *future* means nothing . . . to him."

"Shhhhhh." He rubbed his cheek against the silken crown of her head and drew large, soothing circles on her back.

"Oh, Graham . . . what am I . . . going to do . . . ?"

"We'll fight it, love. He can't do this to us."

"But he will! You didn't . . . hear his voice! I swear he's a madman!"

Sobs wrenched her body anew, tearing Graham apart. Had Jason Barry been there at that moment, he would gladly have strangled the man. Instead, he simply tightened his hold on Debra in an attempt to absorb her pain. Only when her crying began to taper off did he hold her away. Framing her face with his hands, he brushed at her tears with his thumbs, then gently kissed her cheeks.

"Come on," he murmured. "Let's take a walk." Bringing her under the curve of his arm, he led her through the kitchen to the back-yard swing, where he seated her comfortably against him. "Now. Tell me exactly what he said."

"Oh, Graham . . ." she began, and started to cry again.

He held her patiently, offering silent comfort until she'd composed herself once more. "Okay?"

She sniffled, nodded, then took a hiccuping breath. "He said that the divorce wasn't legal. That the notary who vouched for his signature of consent wasn't authorized to do so since his term had expired." Her tears returned, and her fingers clutched at Graham's shirt. "It's not fair!" she cried, her cheeks streaked as she looked up at him in misery. "It's just not fair!"

He let her cry, sensing the outpouring to be an expression of the original hurt that had destroyed her marriage. She needed the release. He was only glad that he was there to hold her. One long leg kept the swing moving gently back and forth. Between the hypnotic motion and its rhythmic creak and the comfort of Graham's strong arms, Debra finally regained control.

"I'm sorry to . . . break down like this."

"Shhhhhh. You've got every right."

"But it doesn't solve anything."

"Sure makes you feel better, though, doesn't it?"

Hearing a smile in his voice, she looked up and forced a weak one of her own. "It does." Then she blotted her eyes. "But where do we go from here? I feel so helpless."

Graham wasn't. "First, you're going to go get the divorce decree and your copy of Jason's letter. You've got it here, haven't you."

She nodded and was up in a flash. When she returned from the carriage house, she had the offending paper in hand. Sliding down next to Graham again, she opened it for them both to see. "He's right," she murmured wretchedly, pointing to the gold seal. "See that date? The seal expired three months before the divorce. Why didn't I *see* that? Why didn't Fuller catch that?"

"Fuller?"

"Paul Fuller. He handled the divorce arrangements for me. I was pretty upset at the time and only knew that I wanted it done and fast. He took care of everything—the plane, the hotel, the contact in Port-au-Prince."

"And who is this Gerald Axhelm?"

"The notary? Who knows! Someone Jason dug up! For all I know, the moron may be a distant relative of his!" Her voice rose. "How could someone do this to us?"

"Take it easy, love." Graham squeezed her hand, then eyed her earnestly. "The first thing to do is to call Paul Fuller. He can get to work on it."

"But what can he do?"

"He can look for a catch. Track down this notary. *Something.*"

"I don't know, Graham. Paul was our lawyer—and friend—when we were married. He's as easily apt to tie things up if Jason's already gotten to him."

"You used Jason's friend to arrange your divorce?"

"But Jason was in total agreement then. Don't you see? He didn't once suggest he'd fight it!" She threw up her hands in a return of dismay. "I can't believe this. I mean, why would he ever want a wife who would hate him?"

"Perhaps it's a matter of principle."

"*Principle?* My God, he's got to be crazy!"

"When he was here that day, you suggested he was going through a midlife crisis. That may well be it, you know. He may be reacting to the knowledge that he's not getting any younger, that he may have hit the peak of his career, of his power."

She eyed him skeptically. "You think so?"

He shrugged. "Not knowing the man, I couldn't say for sure. But it's always a possibility. It makes sense."

"It *doesn't* make sense," Debra exploded perversely. "He has everything going for him. This whole *thing* is bizarre! If I wrote a script like this, Harris would burn it!"

Graham gave a wry chuckle. "There have been times," he drawled, "when I suspected that much of your life smacked of soap opera."

"It doesn't. It can't! At least, that's not what I want," she proclaimed soberly. "This house, this land, you— I've finally found a semblance of sanity." Her throat tightened. "I can't lose it now, Graham," she whispered. "I just can't."

Suddenly sober himself, he hauled her into his arms. "You won't, love. You've got my word on that. Jason can't have it all his way." He thought for a minute. "Listen, let me give *my* lawyer a call."

"You're still in touch with him?"

"He keeps an eye on my investments for me, so I talk with him often. Besides, he's a good friend."

"And you think he could help?"

"He could certainly look into the matter. We don't know the law—it's as simple as that. He does. He'll need to see that paper, and he'll want to talk with you—"

Debra sat up abruptly. Her eyes darkened with a sheen of stubbornness. "I'm not going to New York, Graham. It's out of the question."

"Shhhhhh." He tucked a strand of hair behind her ear. "You may not have to." His voice was deep and smooth, comforting even as it was firm. "For now, you can talk with him on the phone. Later, well, we'll see what he says." He paused. "You know, you can't avoid the city forever."

"Look who's talking," she exclaimed, but any sharpness there might have been was fast falling victim to a returning bleakness.

"*I've* got no reason to return. If Jason's claim is correct and you have to take him to court, *you* may have no choice."

"God, I hope he's wrong. It's got to be a hoax." She scowled. "He must have somehow known you and I had finally—" Her breath caught on that electric thought.

"It'll be all right. You'll see. Come on." Careful to keep his voice light, he took her hand and drew her up. "Let's give Peter a call."

As it happened, Peter wasn't in. Graham did his best, leaving Debra's number and explaining that they'd be there all day, before hanging up the phone.

"I'm sorry, Deb. He'll get back to us as soon as he gets in. I wish I could take you out somewhere to get your mind off this, but we can't stray far from the phone."

"It's all right, Graham," she said dejectedly. "I've got to do some writing, anyway."

"Writing? You're sure you'll be able to work?"

A bitter laugh slipped through her lips. "If I don't get something done, Harris may fire me yet. And besides, writing demands my concentration. It's better than sitting around doing nothing." If she tried *that,* she'd end up watching Graham. And if she did *that,* she'd end up wanting him. Standing on tiptoes now, she linked her arms behind his neck and held tight for a minute. "I love you," she whispered, "and I don't care if it's a sin. Am I horrible?"

His arms enveloped her slender form. "I wouldn't have you any other way," he moaned. Then, drawing his head back, he gave her a long, leisurely, soul-sweeping kiss before sending her off to work.

It was a nightmare of a day, the only solace being that each accomplished more than usual. Graham pounded his nails, Debra her keys. It was sublimation in its most basic form, productivity in exchange for worry.

Having been in court all afternoon, Peter O'Reilly didn't call back until an agonizing five o'clock. He talked first with Graham, then very willingly with Debra, taking down the notary's name and license number for purposes of tracing him. With instructions for her to air express the letter of consent to him in the morning, he gave her as much encouragement as he could, then promised to call at the first sign of news.

That sign didn't come until late the following afternoon, and it was far from promising. The notary, Gerald Axhelm, had been an accountant with a small New York firm but had left under questionable circumstances. A forwarding address seemed to be nonexistent.

"What do we do now?" Debra asked, discouraged.

Peter was far from defeated. "We put an investigator on it. There are several I work with from time to time. The one I have in mind will trace our man. It's just a matter of time."

Time, though, was the enemy, for it brought with it endless brooding. As he had on Thursday night, Graham insisted on spending the weekend with Debra.

"We can't . . ." she had said, teary-eyed and distraught when he led her to bed. Much as she ached for him, the thought of making love to Graham, having learned that she still might be married to another man, was unacceptable. She loved Graham far too much to knowingly cast such a shadow on what they shared.

"I know, love. I know. But we can be close. We can lie together even if we don't make love."

"It'll be torture!"

"Would you rather I leave?"

"No!" That thought was worse. Despite the constant temptation and the fact that the constant need to resist it brought constant recollection of Jason and the upended state of her life, Debra found infinite comfort in Graham's presence.

By night, he held her gently; by day, he kept her not much farther from his side. Often they talked, learning more about each other and their respective pasts; often they worked or simply sat and read together. There were lighter moments, such as the one on Sunday morning. Jogging in with the newspapers he had gotten from their roadside box, Graham helped himself to the *New York Times*, leaving the local press for Debra.

"Hey!" she exclaimed. "What do you think you're doing?"

"Reading the paper," he answered, settling lazily back on the bed in the loft. "I always spend Sunday morning reading the paper."

"But that's *my* paper. Here." She shoved the local news across at him and reached for the *Times*.

He held tight, his eyes full of mischief. "Come on, Deb. Where's that old hospitality?"

"But . . . the *Times*? I thought I was the only one around here who read it."

"If that were true, you'd never have gotten home delivery." He gave a tug. "Come on."

Debra yielded, but only to sit back and study him. Her gaze grew as thoughtful as her voice. "Boy, was I dumb. I should have realized."

"Tired of me already?" he quipped, removing the editorials, then tossing the rest back to her. "I'm not *that* bad. See? I'm perfectly willing to share."

But her mind was elsewhere, two months back in

time. "That first day I met you, you commented that my outfit looked like one you'd seen in an ad for Bloomingdale's or such the Sunday before. Since there's no Bloomingdale's up here, the local papers wouldn't be carrying ads, now, would they? You dropped a clue, and I missed it. I should have known then that you were more than a local carpenter."

Graham seemed infinitely amused. "What can I say? You must have been so blinded by my physical presence that your mind was addled."

She grinned. "You were covered with grease, and your personality left something to be desired. But yes"—she came forward on her knees and put her arms around his neck—"my mind *was* addled. You affected me way back then." Lowering her head, she kissed him softly. "I love you," she whispered, catching her breath when his lips opened to prevent her escape. They were moist and enveloping, parting hers to allow for his tongue's surge into her deepest honeyed recesses. And while his mouth spoke of his love, his hands restlessly roamed her body. When finally he tore himself away, his gaze fell from her lips to her throat, to the lacy bodice of her nightgown.

"This isn't smart," he rasped as his eyes lingered on the rising swells of her breasts before darting up to meet her longing gaze. The muscle in his jaw grew taut. "Peter better come up with something damned fast. I don't know how much more of this I can take."

"I know," she whispered mournfully. "I'm sorry. I shouldn't have started it. It's just that . . . just that . . ." How could she express the depth of her love? To say that she wanted him as much as he wanted her was to tell only half the story. It was in their lovemaking, when his body was deeply embedded in hers, that the other half spilled out. Then they were man and woman, united in an eternal rite of togetherness and hope. Then there was the promise of a tomorrow together, of a time in the future when they might create something that would outlive them both.

Stunned by the course of her thoughts, Debra shrugged dumbly, lifted a portion of the paper, and feigning concentration, leaned silently against the headboard beside Graham. That she might want a child was something she hadn't given much thought to in the past. She'd never considered it with Jason. He was busy and very clearly didn't want to be tied down; she was so wrapped up in *him* that she didn't think twice.

Her relationship with Graham, however, was something else. *Graham* was something else. Whereas Jason had been the sole focus of her relationship with him, the focus of her relationship with Graham seemed to be their love. There was a give-and-take she hadn't known with a man before, a very beautiful sense of sharing both the good and the bad in life. His presence with her now was proof of that, as was the time they'd spent in soul-spilling at his house the other day.

She'd seen the agony in Graham's eyes when he talked of his loss of Jessica. She knew he'd want a child. She also knew he'd adore that child, even as he could adore Debra all the more for bearing it. And the feeling was mutual. She knew she had enough love inside for both Graham *and* his child. Very simply, she wanted that child. Oh, not immediately; there was too much she wanted to do with Graham alone. But certainly at some future time.

Yet even as she thrilled at the thought of it, the weight of her predicament settled on her. There were two problems—the divorce that Jason claimed was nonbinding and Jessica. As for the divorce, she had to believe that even if the Haitian trip proved to have been a fiasco, she'd be able to get her divorce in time. Jessica was another matter. Before Graham fathered another child, he had to work out his feelings about Jessica. That he had told Debra about her was only a sharing of the problem. The problem itself still existed in the depth of guilt and regret, whether justified or not, that Graham felt.

"Are you all right?" His gentle voice, tinged with concern, broke into her thoughts, and she turned to look at him.

"Uh . . . yes." She forced a smile. "I'm okay."

He doubted it, even sensed where her thoughts had been, for his weren't far away. For the time being, though, there was nothing to do but wait. "Come here," he whispered, and stretched out an arm. She accepted his invitation instantly, dropping the paper she hadn't read and curling against him with her cheek on his chest. "See how much I love you," he teased, retrieving the section of the paper he'd been reading. "I'll even share this."

And so they read . . . and waited . . . and worried. As solicitous as Graham was to Debra, and she to him, the tension began to mount. There was physical frustration; they didn't dare make love. Even worse was the psychological strain of wondering what the future held.

By the time Monday morning came, Graham was back to hitting his nails with a vengeance, wondering how his life had suddenly become complicated, yet knowing that he wouldn't have it differently if it meant losing Debra. Debra, in turn, recalled the days she'd envisioned her life here to be quiet and peaceful and knew that suddenly she couldn't picture *any* life here without Graham.

Working with a fury born of frustration, he finished the shingling on Monday and moved indoors on Tuesday. Similarly, Debra produced page after page of script, moving further ahead than she'd ever been simply for need of the escape.

With each ringing of the phone, both heads turned, both hearts raced. With each false alarm, twin hopes fell. When the right call finally came late Wednesday afternoon, it was a breath-stopping moment for them both.

"It's all right, then?" Graham said when emotion prevented Debra from speaking. Their heads were side by side, his lowered, hers raised, their ears sharing the phone.

"It's fine!" Peter exclaimed in triumph. "We located Axhelm in Oregon. It seems that he left the firm in New York for personal reasons. His fiancée had been going through a bad time with her family and had to return to Portland. They were having all sorts of problems trying to decide what to do. His work suffered. When the two other partners confronted him, he up and quit on the spot. There were some unkind words said and some negative feelings all around; hence, the firm's refusal to hand out a forwarding address."

"But the seal," Graham prompted. "Is it good?"

"The seal itself? No. It *had* expired. But that's irrelevant. He's still a notary. He did renew his license even if he forgot to order a new seal."

"Then Jason's signature is binding?" Graham slipped his arm around Debra's waist and drew her even closer. She trembled in anticipation.

"It is indeed."

"And there's no chance that Axhelm's lying, trying to cover for a slip?" Graham wanted no stone left unturned this time.

"Nope. I had my man check out his credentials *and* his notary's certificate. He's clean. The divorce is perfectly legitimate. As soon as I hang up the phone, I'll dictate a letter to that intent and have it sent by messenger to Barry. He'll have it tonight."

"Thank you, Peter," Debra managed to get out. Her eyes were filled with tears of relief. She felt light and free and incredibly happy.

"Thanks, pal." Graham echoed her sentiment. "I do appreciate all you've done." As appreciative as he was, he couldn't get Peter off the phone fast enough. "Thank God!" he said then, all but throwing the instrument to the floor before closing his arms around Debra. A tremor passed through his limbs as he buried his face in her hair. "Thank God!"

Debra wasn't sure which made her happier—Peter's news or Graham's resultant relief. She knew that during the time she'd been so distressed, Graham had been strong and reassuring. Only now did she understand the extent of his strain. In its wake, she felt wanted and loved, more so than she'd ever felt in her life.

It seemed only natural that they should make love right there on the living-room floor. Having endured six days of hell, they owed it to each other. Without a word spoken, clothes were torn off and tossed to the side. When their bare flesh finally touched, it was with a sense of awe, with a greater appreciation than either had had before. Lips locked in a hungry kiss, they sank to the floor and knelt before one another. Feeling, touching, exploring—all were permissible, none deniable.

Graham rediscovered every part of her body, loving each with his hands, then his mouth, while she sighed his name and arched her back in bliss. Yet she, too, was greedy. Her eager hands raced over him, measuring the swell of his shoulders and chest, savoring the leanness of his waist and hips, loving the texture of him from the broad mat of hair on his chest to the pencil-thin line at his navel, then lower.

As her fingers closed around his hardness, his found her warmth and stroked its velvet softness until, unable to endure his sweet torture, she guided him to her. With a show of the physical power she found so exciting, he slid his hands beneath her thighs and lifted her against him. When he drew her legs farther apart to circle his hips, she locked her ankles together at the base of his spine. Then, easily bearing both their weights, he leaned forward and lowered her to the floor.

What happened next was an experience in eroticism far beyond anything Debra had ever imagined. Her body ceased to exist except as a vital part of his, rising with and against it in perfect harmony. From their point of joining irradiated a star burst of sensation, one spangle more fiery than the next, each progressively hotter until they converged on a pinnacle of ecstasy and exploded.

"Gra . . . ham . . ." she gasped in a fractured voice as the blinding spasms went on and on.

"I . . . know," he moaned, his body pulsating in her, his heart throbbing on her. He moaned again as the quaking subsided, then, without withdrawing, rolled them to their sides and crushed her trembling body to his. "I'll never let you go, Debra. So help me, I won't!"

At the sound of his fierce possessiveness, she recalled the lion she'd thought him once. He was strong and stately, a king among men. And she positively adored him.

"What are you thinking?" he whispered by her ear, fanning it with his breath, then licking its shell-like curve.

She gasped and buried her face against the damp, musky skin of his neck. "I was thinking that I'd . . . follow you anywhere."

"How about to dinner tonight, someplace nice to celebrate?"

"Mmmmmm. I'd . . . like . . . that."

It sounded heavenly. Much later, after Graham had left to return to his house to clean up and change, she showered and dressed in the white silk he'd loved so much. Singing softly as she caught her hair up with a silken clip, she felt gay and lighthearted. This was the first day of the rest of their lives. They'd managed to survive her ordeal with Jason; when the time was right, Graham's problem concerning Jessica would also be solved. The future seemed bright and alive, until she opened the door to an ashen-faced Graham and knew that something was very much amiss.

"What is it?" she gasped, eyes widening on the shirt that hung loose over his jeans. He'd neither shaved nor showered and stood in a pose of utter depression. His time had obviously been spent in hell. "What's the matter?" Her heart nearly stopped in fear.

Graham looked at her distractedly. "Maybe . . . maybe I shouldn't have come . . ." he mumbled, but she'd put her hand on his arm before he could turn and leave.

"What's wrong? Tell me, Graham!" she cried, suddenly shadowed by an overwhelming fear.

He thrust a hand through his hair, as he must have done a dozen times in the past hour. "The phone was ringing when I got home." He paused, as though saying the words made them all the more real, all the more excruciating.

"Yes . . . ?" Debra coaxed in a frightened whisper.

"It was my father. He's been trying to reach me since yesterday morning." Again, he paused, took a breath, then looked straight at Debra. "It's Jessie. She's been hurt."

Debra sucked in her breath sharply. "What happened?"

"A cab barreled around a corner and hit her while she was running across the street."

"My God, Graham! How bad is it?"

It took him a minute before he was able to answer. "Dad wasn't sure. He received a quick call from Joan. The fact that she called at all says something for the seriousness of it. Jessie was on the operating table for a good part of last night. There were some broken bones and internal injuries. They think they've stopped the bleeding now, but she's still in critical condition."

Stepping closer, Debra raised her hands to his shoulders. "I'm so sorry, Graham." Her arms slid around his neck, and she settled close to him. "Is there . . . is there anything I can do?"

He was even longer in answering this time. But his arms had curved around her back, and she felt him absorbing her comfort. "I don't know . . . I don't think so." Then, with a sigh, he drew back to look at her. "I've got to go down, Debra. This is my chance. She may never know I was there, but I don't think I'd forgive myself if I didn't try."

Through the depth of her distress, Debra felt a surge of pride. Graham Reid was quite a man. Stretching up, she kissed him lightly. "I don't think you would, either. . . . When do you want to leave?"

"I've already called. There's nothing going out tonight, but there is an early flight from Manchester tomorrow that will put me in the city by ten." He hesitated, then eyed her apologetically. "I . . . uh . . . Do you mind if we postpone dinner? I don't think I'd be very good company."

"Of course I don't mind. Why don't we go back to your place in case your dad calls again. If you're hungry, I can fix you something there."

"You're sure you don't mind?" His gaze fell to her dress, and his voice lowered. "You look so pretty."

Feeling positively cherished by the look of love in his eyes, she fought to keep her voice from breaking. "I can wear it another time," she said as she gently disengaged herself from him. "Just give me a minute to change and pack."

He frowned. "Pack?"

"I'm going with you."

She heard the sharp intake of his breath and saw the look of disbelief on his face. "To New York?" She nodded, and the simple gesture touched him deeply, giving his voice a ragged edge. "You don't have to do that, Deb. I know how much you detest the thought."

She moved closer again and took his hand, raising it to her lips, then pressing it to her cheek. "The thought I detest is of your going alone. I want to be with you, Graham. Unless . . . of course, unless you'd rather I didn't . . ."

"Oh, Debra . . ." Her name flowed in a deep breath, carrying a bit of his soul along with it. Reaching out, he took her face in his hands and lowered his own to meet it. His lips were gentle and loving. "Oh, Debra . . . what did I ever do to deserve you? You'd really go back there with me?"

"Yes," she whispered with all her heart.

He kissed her deeply then, leaving no doubt as to his love and thanks. With Debra by his side, he felt a strange optimism. Jessica would be all right. She had to be. There were too many things he had to say to her. He'd do it slowly, as David French had done. But he was determined to take that first step.

They left at dawn to drive down to Manchester, caught the plane and arrived in New York, as Graham had promised, by ten. Neither said much during the trip. Their intertwined hands expressed an awareness of one another, a need to know that the other was there.

Having been so thoroughly determined not to return, Debra was surprised at her inner calm. But she was a different woman now from the broken one who had left over two months before. Her proof was Graham, by her side, giving her confidence, taking confidence from her. He needed her more than any other human being had ever needed her, and she felt that much more of a person for it.

They took a cab from the airport to the hospital, where Debra waited downstairs while a grim-faced Graham went up. She sat for what seemed an eternity, though it was only a matter of hours. When he returned at last, he was pale and wan, but he smiled so very gently that she knew he was at peace.

She said nothing, simply took the hand he held out to her. Still without a word, they headed uptown. When he directed the cabbie to pull up at the Plaza, she cast him a questioning glance. His pallor had begun to recede, and a hint of spirit played in his eyes.

"We need *somewhere* to stay," he answered her silent query, then said no more as he paid the driver and entrusted their bags to an elegant-liveried doorman.

For the first time since their plane had touched down at LaGuardia, Debra felt the reality of her return. The Plaza *was* New York, sophisticated, elegant, romantic. Yet, walking up the red-carpeted steps toward the huge revolving doors, she was a visitor. The city was her home no more; her heart lay elsewhere.

Looking up, she caught Graham's eye and smiled shyly. Strange, she mused, but she felt a bit like the country girl visiting the city for the first time. Her clothes, a chic linen suit and high-heeled sandals, seemed foreign to her body, though she wore them with the same flair she always had. Graham's gaze confirmed that.

"You okay?" he whispered, tucking her hand under his elbow as they approached the registration desk.

"Uh-huh," she replied in a wispy tone, gaining confidence from him once more. But he was tired. She could see it in spite of the smile he managed for her. It had been a long day, an even longer night before. He'd barely slept. She'd spent much of her own night watching him toss and turn. Now, watching him in concern, she knew he needed rest.

The bellboy had no sooner showed them to their room, deposited their bags and closed the door behind them than Graham shrugged out of his jacket, tossed it on a chair and began to tug at his tie. Without a word, Debra took the jacket and hung it up, turning to find that he'd collapsed onto the bed, his long legs stretched before him, an arm thrown across his eyes. She tossed her own jacket aside with nearly as much care as he'd taken, stepped out of her shoes and sat on the edge of the bed beside him.

"Can I get you anything, Graham?" she asked softly. "An aspirin, some water, room service?"

His arm left his eyes to settle over her shoulders and draw her down. "No, love. Just you. Just a couple of minutes of quiet."

She curled easily against him, her body fine tuned to his masculine lines. Her cheek rested against the smooth cotton of his shirt. She laid her arm along his fine leather belt. Much as she wanted to hear what had happened in the hospital, she knew that he needed these moments of regeneration first.

His heart beat steadily by her ear in the rhythmic pulse of life. "She's going to be all right," he said at last, expending a deep breath of relief that the word was out.

"Thank God," Debra murmured. Turning her head, she propped her chin on his chest so she could see his face. His eyes were closed, long spiky lashes crowning his cheekbone. "You spoke with the doctors?"

"Yes. They were encouraging. She's broken a leg and an arm, plus several ribs. It was the internal injuries that had them worried. But they feel they've repaired everything, and she seems to be stabilizing. They'll keep her in intensive care for another day or so as a precaution."

Though his voice fell away, Debra's thoughts moved on. "Did you . . . see her?" she whispered more tentatively.

She saw him swallow hard. "Yes. I sat by her bedside most of the time I was there." There was a long silence. Debra noted the way his brows knit as he struggled to express himself. He kept his eyes closed. "It was an . . . an awful feeling," he gasped painfully. His fingers tightened on her shoulder. "So many bandages. She seemed so small. So pale."

In a gesture of comfort, Debra reached up to comb the hair gently from his brow. His skin was warm and firm. She ran her hand down his cheek before finally resting it against his throat, where he'd released the top two buttons of his shirt. Slowly, he opened his eyes, and she saw that they sparkled with unshed tears.

"It was awful, Debra," he rasped. "I haven't seen her in all these years, and I know she's grown up. But I kept seeing the skinny little girl with the long, flowing hair who had fallen off her bike and cut her knee. But a Band-Aid and a kiss were useless. I couldn't even take her in my arms and hold her. I wanted to do something, but there wasn't a damned thing I could do. She was hurt so badly, and I was totally helpless." He closed his eyes and sniffed. Debra reached up to wipe a lone tear that escaped from the corner of his eye. She left her hand to caress his temple lightly.

"Was she in pain?"

"They'd given her painkillers, so I don't think she felt much of anything. She slept most of the time."

"Then you didn't . . . you didn't talk to her?"

He reached to take her hand and brought it to his lips. She felt his breath against her finger tips when he spoke. "I did. She was surprisingly lucid at times."

"What did she say?"

Graham opened his eyes then and gave a short laugh. "I think I scared the hell out of her."

"What do you mean?"

"The first time she opened her eyes, she stared at me as though I were a three-eyed monster. I guess she couldn't handle it, so she simply went back to sleep. The second time, though, she couldn't deny my presence."

"She recognized you, didn't she?"

He shot her a glance that bore the slightest twist of wry humor. "Oh, yes. She recognized me. . . . She wanted to know if she'd died."

"Oh, no . . . !"

"Oh, yes," he drawled. "When I assured her she hadn't, she assumed I was there because she was *going* to. When I assured her she wasn't, she straight out asked why I'd come." His expression sobered instantly. "Sassy kid."

Debra knew it had to be her own heart thudding so loudly, since Graham seemed to have regained his composure. "What did you say?"

"I decided to sass her right back. I very boldly informed her that she was my daughter and that I loved her."

"And what did she say?"

"Nothing. She stared at me for a little while longer, then closed her eyes and went back to sleep."

"Then what happened?" Debra felt as though she were hanging on the edge of a precipice, with Graham deliberately letting her dangle.

"She woke up a few minutes later. I didn't know what in the hell to do. I was afraid that if I said too much, I'd only upset her. And God only knows she's got enough to deal with right now."

"So what did you do?"

"I just sat there."

"You didn't say anything?"

"No. I had said the only things that really mattered. I figured she was old enough to take it from there."

"And did she?"

His chest expanded beneath her chin when he took a deep breath. "Not at first. She dozed on and off for a little while, waking up each time with her eyes on me. I think she expected me to just . . . vanish at some point. The fact that I didn't must have made its point." He grew suspiciously hoarse. "The next time she woke up, she actually smiled. . . . The time after that, she . . . she inched her hand toward me." His voice broke, and he had to pause. This time, Debra couldn't see his eyes glistening. Her own were flooded. "I just sat there for a while, holding her hand until the nurse came to see to her. Then I left."

It was a long time before either spoke again, a time of rest and renewal. Debra felt so happy for Graham. He seemed so satisfied. It was only a beginning. Both knew that. But suddenly there was time and hope.

She wasn't sure who dozed first, she or Graham. When she awoke, though, it was late afternoon, and Graham was waiting. "I was worried you'd sleep forever, and I didn't have the heart to wake you."

"You should have! Have you been up long?"

Shifting onto his side, he pressed her close. His hand slid the length of her spine to arch her body to his. "Long enough to get all hot and bothered looking at you," he growled, then gave a moan and crushed her even closer. One long leg slid intimately between hers. "Ahhhhh, Debra, do you have any idea how much I love you?"

She smiled coyly. "I've got a pretty good idea how much you *want* me."

He cocked an eye wide at her pertness. "You have, have you?"

There was no doubt. The pressure against her thigh had already begun to stir similar yearnings in her. "Uh-huh."

To her surprise, he released her abruptly and rolled to

the far side of the bed and up in one fluid surge, then strode around the bed until he stood towering above her. His head was high, his shoulders straight. There was something decidedly arrogant in his stance, marginally mischievous, utterly masculine. His hair gleamed its rich tawny shade in the late-afternoon sunlight that glanced into the room. He was the lion personified; her insides quivered in excitement.

His relentless eyes held hers as, one by one, he slowly stripped the clothes from his body. His shirt went first, tugged from his pants, unbuttoned, peeled from his shoulders to reveal that broad, bronzed chest whose feel and taste and smell she knew so well. His hands then went to his belt, releasing its buckle, drawing it from its loops with a deliberation that was matched by the fingers that grasped his zipper tab and inched it firmly down. Debra's temperature rose as he kicked off his loafers, then stepped from his pants. When he stood before her in nothing but his briefs, she caught her breath. When he hooked his thumbs under their waistband and eased them over his hips, she felt a sensual vibration pulsate through her body.

He was magnificent, tall, lean and fully aroused. His body was an amalgam of textures, ranging from the roughened plane of his chest to the paler, smoother skin of his hips. A mass of sinewed parts, he wore his work well. With the casting off of his city clothes, he was her carpenter again, the physical, earthy, ruggedly handsome man she loved.

His ravenous amber gaze raked her fully clothed body. "Take them off," he growled half in play, half in earnest. It was to the latter that Debra responded, finding the strength from it to force her quivering limbs to support her as she slipped from the bed and began to undress. Her blouse and skirt went first, falling to the floor and fast forgotten. Increasingly aroused herself, yet self-conscious under Graham's intent gaze, she slid her slip more hesitantly down her legs, moistened her lips, then let her pantyhose follow.

Standing before him in only twin wisps of lace, she wavered while queer little tingles fluttered in the pit of her stomach. As naked and unselfconscious as he was, she felt astoundingly shy. He was the consummate hero, larger than life, his body primed for her taking. And his eyes saw everything, devouring her even now.

"The bra first," he ordered thickly.

Swallowing hard in a struggle for composure, she raised shaking hands to her back. It took her a minute to release the hook. Slowly, she pulled the delicate fabric from her breasts and set their fullness free.

Graham took a small step forward. His breathing was unsteady now, giving Debra the courage to look at him. To know that she could arouse the lion so completely was heady knowledge, indeed.

His eyes caressed her creaminess, drawing her nipples up tight before searing a path between her breasts to her navel, then lower. "Now those," he ordered in a deep, rasping tone, jutting his chin toward the triangular bit of silk.

An electrifying shimmer coursed through her veins. For a minute, she couldn't move.

"The panties, Debra." Timidly, she shimmied the sleek fabric over her hips and down her legs, then forced herself to stand before him, as naked now as he. "That's better," he growled. With a flick of his wrist, he turned back the bedspread. His command was softened only by a gentle tug at the corner of his mouth. "Now lie down."

Debra's entire body felt afire. She'd never experienced anything as thoroughly provocative as Graham's dominance. It was as though he, too, needed a reminder of that other life, that simpler, more physical and lusty life they'd left behind at dawn.

"Lie down!" he said more harshly. But she knew him

too well to be afraid. His muscles trembled. His chest skin bore a fine sheen of sweat. He was on the verge of losing control, and she reveled in the thought.

With careful movements, she sat on the edge of the bed, then inched toward its center and slowly lowered her body until she lay flat on her back, looking up at Graham. Had she not known him so well, she might have been frightened by the sheer sense of power exuded by his firm, athletic body. Had she not trusted him so much, she might have been frightened by the raw size of him. But she loved him and she knew that he'd never, never hurt her. And her body craved his with such sizzling intensity that she had no choice but to accept whatever sweet torment he had in store.

Round-eyed, she watched as he came to the edge of the bed, ran smoldering eyes from her shoulder to her thighs and back, then put one knee on the mattress and swung the other over her legs. Straddling her body, he propped his fists beneath her arms. Then, his eyes heavy lidded, he savored her pose, finding satisfaction in the rapid rise and fall of her breasts, finding pleasure in the way she bit her lip to keep from crying out for him. Bending his head low with infinite leisure, he brought his mouth to within a breath of hers, teasing her with the promise of a fiery kiss, coaxing her lips open again and again, never quite touching her. He was taken off guard when her fingers suddenly clutched the hair on his chest.

"Graham! I can't stand this!" she wailed, arching upward in search of satisfaction. The gaze that met hers was instantly soft.

"You mean . . . all this . . . and I didn't scare you . . . even a little?"

"Scare me? My God, Graham," she gasped, "I need you so badly that nothing you do could *possibly* scare me!"

"Nothing?" he asked with such smugness that she

grew instantly wary. When he sat up straight and started off the bed, she'd had it.

"I was wrong!" she cried, bolting up and after him. *"That* scares me!" She coiled her arms around his neck, prepared to hang on forever. "Don't ever leave me," she whispered. "I don't think I could bear it!"

With an answering groan, he clutched her tightly, pressing flesh to flesh in thorough intimacy. "I couldn't leave you, love. You're my better half. Don't you know that?" Any answer she might have made was lost in his mouth as it closed over hers and ravaged her to mindlessness. Only when he freed her to bury his face in the softness of her neck did she speak.

"You are a pussycat, Graham," she whispered with a smile.

"A pussycat?" he growled, sounding suspiciously like the lion. "A *pussycat?"* With a deep animal sound from the back of his throat, he tumbled her to the bed and drove deeply, taking her with a ferocity that excited her all the more. If ever there'd been violence in their mating, it was there now, a raw expression of the force of their love. Nothing was one-sided. When Graham nipped the ivory warmth of her shoulder, she dug her nails into the sun-baked flesh of his back. When Debra tightened herself to hold him in, he moved all the more forcefully. It was a passionate battle for the title of the most ardent. Yet when the final explosion had struck in mind-shattering ecstasy, leaving their bodies sweat slickened and spent, there was no loser in sight.

Long after, Graham reached for the phone. "Champagne and caviar for room 3433, please."

"Champagne and caviar?" Debra murmured against his chest.

He replaced the receiver and grinned down at her. "We deserve it, wouldn't you say? It's been a rough week." He flicked on the bedside radio to cushion them in the soft sounds of easy listening. Then, fitting her more snugly to his manly mold, he clasped his arms around her back and spoke gently. "I'd like to stop by the hospital again tonight. Would you mind? We could go out for a late dinner after that."

"Of course I don't mind! That sounds perfect."

A soft sigh of satisfaction flitted from his lips across her brow. "I want to spend a few days here . . . to make sure she's all right . . . to make sure she knows I've got no intention of letting her go again. Can you . . . would you stay here with me? I mean, I know you've got work to do."

"The work will wait. Besides, thanks to pure nervous energy, I've gotten so far ahead in the last week that I can easily spare the time." She tipped her head back against his shoulder. "I may even go over to the studio and catch up on the tapes of the shows I've missed."

"You'd want to do that?" he asked cautiously. He knew how humiliated she'd felt at one point, how the thought of seeing her coworkers intimidated her.

But she smiled with the confidence he'd given her. "I think I could now. I think I'd like to. I want all that behind me when we go home."

Graham's arms tightened, and his lips touched her nose. When she strained upward, he caught her mouth with delicate precision, expressing his pride in a wordless caress. When once more she snuggled down against him, they both closed their eyes to relish the moment.

Just then, the haunting lilt of an old country ballad wafted into the air. Though there was no voice to detract from the melodious strains of violin and cello, the words returned to her with poignant clarity, words about a carpenter and his lady, a marriage, a baby.

Debra opened her eyes to find Graham staring at her with that quiet intensity she found so disarming.

"You will, won't you?" he asked, his voice deep and urgent.

"Yes," she whispered, her heart brimming.

"The baby part, too?"

She caught her breath, eyes wide with joy. "You're sure?"

The look on his face spoke of a love that could conquer all. "Never more sure of anything in my life," he murmured, then kissed her to seal the vow.

15-Day Free Trial Offer
6 Silhouette Romances

6 Silhouette Romances, free for 15 days! We'll send you 6 new Silhouette Romances to keep for 15 days, absolutely free! If you decide not to keep them, send them back to us. You pay nothing.

Free Home Delivery. But if you enjoy them as much as we think you will, keep them by paying the invoice enclosed with your free trial shipment. We'll pay all shipping and handling charges. You get the convenience of Home Delivery and we pay the postage and handling charge each month.

Don't miss a copy. The Silhouette Book Club is the way to make sure you'll be able to receive every new romance we publish before they're sold out. There is no minimum number of books to buy and you can cancel at any time.

This offer expires July 31, 1984

Silhouette Book Club, Dept. SRSE 7L
120 Brighton Road, Clifton, NJ 07012

Please send me 6 Silhouette Romances to keep for 15 days, absolutely free. I understand I am not obligated to join the Silhouette Book Club unless I decide to keep them.

NAME_____

ADDRESS_____

CITY_____ STATE_____ ZIP_____

MORE ROMANCE FOR
A SPECIAL WAY TO RELAX
$1.95 each

2 ☐ Hastings	23 ☐ Charles	45 ☐ Charles	66 ☐ Mikels
3 ☐ Dixon	24 ☐ Dixon	46 ☐ Howard	67 ☐ Shaw
4 ☐ Vitek	25 ☐ Hardy	47 ☐ Stephens	68 ☐ Sinclair
5 ☐ Converse	26 ☐ Scott	48 ☐ Ferrell	69 ☐ Dalton
6 ☐ Douglass	27 ☐ Wisdom	49 ☐ Hastings	70 ☐ Clare
7 ☐ Stanford	28 ☐ Ripy	50 ☐ Browning	71 ☐ Skillern
8 ☐ Halston	29 ☐ Bergen	51 ☐ Trent	72 ☐ Belmont
9 ☐ Baxter	30 ☐ Stephens	52 ☐ Sinclair	73 ☐ Taylor
10 ☐ Thiels	31 ☐ Baxter	53 ☐ Thomas	74 ☐ Wisdom
11 ☐ Thornton	32 ☐ Douglass	54 ☐ Hohl	75 ☐ John
12 ☐ Sinclair	33 ☐ Palmer	55 ☐ Stanford	76 ☐ Ripy
13 ☐ Beckman	35 ☐ James	56 ☐ Wallace	77 ☐ Bergen
14 ☐ Keene	36 ☐ Dailey	57 ☐ Thornton	78 ☐ Gladstone
15 ☐ James	37 ☐ Stanford	58 ☐ Douglass	79 ☐ Hastings
16 ☐ Carr	38 ☐ John	59 ☐ Roberts	80 ☐ Douglass
17 ☐ John	39 ☐ Milan	60 ☐ Thorne	81 ☐ Thornton
18 ☐ Hamilton	40 ☐ Converse	61 ☐ Beckman	82 ☐ McKenna
19 ☐ Shaw	41 ☐ Halston	62 ☐ Bright	83 ☐ Major
20 ☐ Musgrave	42 ☐ Drummond	63 ☐ Wallace	84 ☐ Stephens
21 ☐ Hastings	43 ☐ Shaw	64 ☐ Converse	85 ☐ Beckman
22 ☐ Howard	44 ☐ Eden	65 ☐ Cates	86 ☐ Halston

Silhouette Special Edition

87 ☐ Dixon	101 ☐ Bergen	115 ☐ Halston	129 ☐ Rowe
88 ☐ Saxon	102 ☐ Wallace	116 ☐ Roberts	130 ☐ Carr
89 ☐ Meriwether	103 ☐ Taylor	117 ☐ Converse	131 ☐ Lee
90 ☐ Justin	104 ☐ Wallace	118 ☐ Jackson	132 ☐ Dailey
91 ☐ Stanford	105 ☐ Sinclair	119 ☐ Langan	133 ☐ Douglass
92 ☐ Hamilton	106 ☐ John	120 ☐ Dixon	134 ☐ Ripy
93 ☐ Lacey	107 ☐ Ross	121 ☐ Shaw	135 ☐ Seger
94 ☐ Barrie	108 ☐ Stephens	122 ☐ Walker	136 ☐ Scott
95 ☐ Doyle	109 ☐ Beckman	123 ☐ Douglass	137 ☐ Parker
96 ☐ Baxter	110 ☐ Browning	124 ☐ Mikels	138 ☐ Thornton
97 ☐ Shaw	111 ☐ Thorne	125 ☐ Cates	
98 ☐ Hurley	112 ☐ Belmont	126 ☐ Wildman	
99 ☐ Dixon	113 ☐ Camp	127 ☐ Taylor	
100 ☐ Roberts	114 ☐ Ripy	128 ☐ Macomber	

LOOK FOR SHINING HOUR BY PAT WALLACE AVAILABLE IN FEBRUARY AND A LOVESONG AND YOU BY LINDA SHAW IN MARCH.

SILHOUETTE SPECIAL EDITION, Department SE/2
1230 Avenue of the Americas
New York, NY 10020

Please send me the books I have checked above. I am enclosing $_____
(please add 75¢ to cover postage and handling. NYS and NYC residents please
add appropriate sales tax). Send check or money order—no cash or C.O.D.'s
please. Allow six weeks for delivery.

NAME _____

ADDRESS _____

CITY _____ STATE/ZIP _____